Personalising Learning
in the Primary School

Personalising Learning

in the Primary School

DR ELAINE WILMOT

Crown House Publishing Limited
www.crownhouse.co.uk

If you want to feel secure, do what you already know how to do. If you want to be a true professional and continue to grow ... go to the cutting edge of your competence, which means a temporary loss of security. So whenever you don't quite know what you're doing, know that you are growing.

– MADELINE HUNTER

First published by

Crown House Publishing Ltd
Crown Buildings, Bancyfelin, Carmarthen, Wales, SA33 5ND, UK
www.crownhouse.co.uk

and

Crown House Publishing Company LLC
6 Trowbridge Drive, Suite 5, Bethel, CT 06801, USA
www.crownhousepublishing.com

British Library of Cataloguing-in-Publication Data
A catalogue entry for this book is available from the British Library.

International Standard Book Number
10-digit ISBN 1845900030
13-digit ISBN 978-1845900038

Library of Congress Control Number
2006923068

Edited by Bill Lucas
Project management: Janice BaitonEditorial Services, Cambridge
Design and typesetting: Paul Barrett Book Production, Cambridge
Cartoon illustrations: Caroline Matthews

Printed and bound in the UK by *Gomer Press, Llandysul, Ceredigion*

Contents

Preface

As I meet teachers and others who work in education, I am not amazed to find that many people working in schools today had a bad experience of our education system themselves. Many of them were unhappy at school and suffered at the hands of their teachers (either knowingly or unwittingly).

I went through my own school career being told, repeatedly, that I was not good at learning, so I didn't put any effort into the process because what was the point? Consequently, I grew up with a poor self-image of myself as a learner. It was this that inspired me to become a teacher myself so that the children of the then future would not experience the same 'failures' that I had.

I have given this much thought in my adult working life and have come to the conclusion that I 'failed' at school because I was being pushed through a system that was not interested in my own individual learning needs. No one ever took the time to find out how I learned best and consider me as an individual with some strengths and abilities as well as the many areas I had that needed to be developed. Instead, teachers seemed to be able to see only my deficiencies and, because I could not easily commit things to memory and regurgitate them during exams, I was not deemed to be a success at school. What I needed was a system that would start with what I could do and encourage me to build on it, supporting my development as an independent and confident learner – a system of individualising or personalising learning (or PL).

What better way to influence what happens in classrooms and schools than to become a teacher, and eventually a headteacher? So that was what I did, spending thirty years working in schools, seventeen years as a headteacher in three very different schools, trying to ensure that all children got a better chance at being effective learners than I did.

I have spent much of my career in schools researching further this phenomenon of individualised or personalising learning and have come across many able children who were not seen as such until someone took the trouble to get to the core of them and began to understand the way they thought, felt and learned.

I have seen children and staff 'blossom' just by being celebrated for who they are and what they can offer, and they have often told me that they have surprised themselves by achieving what they have just because someone took the time to believe in them and the possibilities of what they could become.

This book will be a practical guide to introducing personalising learning into a primary school, drawing on my seventeen years' experience as a headteacher and on a case study of my last school, where we decided to put PL at the centre of our agenda since the school opened in September 1998. The principle that guided all the work of the school was that the curriculum would be made to fit the child rather than the child being pushed through a prescribed curriculum.

I hope you will find it useful.

Acknowledgements

My heartfelt thanks go to all those I have learned from throughout my career, particularly the many talented and selfless professionals with whom I have had the privilege to work but most particularly the children from whom I have learned so much.

I give special thanks to Bill for his patience, to Caroline for her wonderful cartoons and to Paul and Matthew who have provided undying love and support.

CHAPTER 1

What is Personalising Learning?

Perhaps it would be best to start by saying what personalised learning is not. It is not about abdicating, as teacher, the responsibility of planning and delivering learning activities and the assessment of your pupils. It is not about allowing pupils to do exactly what they want, when they want, how they want, if they want. It is not about a return to the 'laissez-faire' attitudes of the 1960s.

It is about focusing attention on what makes effective learning for every individual learner within your institution, at child (and adult) level and making provision accordingly. It is a shift in emphasis from examining the quality of teaching to looking at how we can provide quality learning. It is a shift in emphasis from curriculum content at the centre to the child's development as a confident and competent learner at the centre of the learning process (this will entail looking at the development of the whole child and not just their cognitive development).

Traditional education in this country is built around a one-size-fits-all model. The curriculum is fixed and delivered in a particular style and the pupils are tested at the end of the system in order to grade their ability (or inability) at regurgitating facts and formulae. My model of PL shifts the starting block from the curriculum to the child and what they can do, and then builds upon their skills at learning and abilities to learn, supporting them in tailoring a curriculum to fit their developing needs.

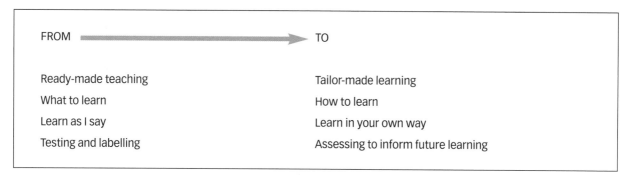

FROM ⟶	TO
Ready-made teaching	Tailor-made learning
What to learn	How to learn
Learn as I say	Learn in your own way
Testing and labelling	Assessing to inform future learning

Figure 1.1

Because what is learning for, anyway? Are we in the business of merely schooling our pupils so that they can ensure that we do well in the league tables? Or are we in the business of preparing them for their lives in a future that is shifting faster than we can keep up with? We need to be moving away from a curriculum based on subject knowledge to a skills-based curriculum, so that our children are prepared for all possible futures.

We should be making the learning fit the learner and not what seems to have been the shift in focus in the education system in the last fifteen years with the advent of the National Curriculum – making the learner fit the learning. As much as we want all our pupils to succeed as learners, we are in a situation in our current system whereby we are still producing too many who are seen as 'failures' because they are unable to access the curriculum for a myriad of reasons. Pupils are opting out because they see the current curriculum and ways of learning as irrelevant to them and their world.

We need our children to be successful as learners but we can't do the learning for them. They must construct their own meaning through their interactions with their environment and other learners around them. We can guide and coach, mentor and support and provide a rich, stimulating environment in which learners can learn and provide an abundance of opportunities for learning, but we can't learn for them. Therefore, we need to examine more closely how we can make learning more accessible to all of our learners.

For me personalising learning is about:

- teachers, or other learning facilitators, knowing each of their learners as an individual;
- knowing each learner's strengths and areas that need further development;
- sharing that knowledge with the learners, through constructive feedback so that they begin to understand themselves as learners and develop the language to describe their learning needs;
- working alongside the child, devolving some of the responsibility for their learning, increasing their independence, over the period of time that the child is in formal schooling;
- supporting children and encouraging them to develop the skills of lifelong learning;
- the teacher (or learning facilitator) really knowing her pupils, as individual people as well as individual learners because learning is about the whole child, not just their cognitive abilities;
- not being a 'slave' to a curriculum, of whomever's design, but working with pupils to create a flexible learning path that will meet their changing needs as they develop;

- looking at systems within our schools to ensure that they provide the flexibility to ensure that we can meet individual needs;
- extending learning beyond the five-plus hours a day for 190 days per year spent in a school – it's about 24/7 learning; and
- trying to do our best for every single child and supporting them in being the best they can be; but
- most of all it is about not tolerating failure for our children.

Our ultimate aim should be for learners to become responsible for managing their own learning and assessment; they should be able to describe themselves in terms of their learning attributes and should be forever seeking new opportunities to develop themselves as learners – learning from their mistakes and from working closely with others.

Knowing how to learn, understanding how to understand and learning how to learn are at the heart of the key skills for lifelong learning. It is not just about mastering a few study skills: it is more about developing a set of positive attitudes to learning.

Where has the notion of personalising learning come from?

The notion of personalising learning first appeared in the public arena in a party conference speech made by Prime Minister Tony Blair in autumn 2003. It was then developed in a speech by David Milliband, then a minister of state, at the National College for School Leadership in October 2003:

> The goal is clear. It is what the prime minister described in his party conference speech as 'personalised learning': an education system where assessment, curriculum, teaching style, and out of hours provision are all designed to discover and nurture the unique talents of every single pupil … the most effective teaching depends on really knowing the needs, strengths and weaknesses of individual pupils.

Personalised learning is seen by the prime minister as part of the wider political context of the personalisation of all public services. It is supported by the advent of 'Every Child Matters' (DfES, 2003a) and 'Excellence and Enjoyment' (DfES, 2003b), where a focus on individual children is pushed to the fore in both documents. Personalisation is also at the heart of the new 'Five-Year Strategy' from the DfES (2004a) and in the White Paper (DfES, 2005).

The 'New Relationship with Schools' (DfES, 2004c) also supports and underpins these initiatives. The government is proposing a cluster of interlocking changes that will affect school inspection, schools' relations with local and central government, schools' self-evaluation and planning, data collection from schools and communication with schools.

But it is not only policy and the legislative framework that are being developed to support personalisation. We are also beginning to see that it is impacting in other areas that affect schools. For example, the National College for School Leadership is starting to develop resources to support personalised learning; the Schools for the Future initiative is looking at building design to accommodate these new ways of working; the National Remodelling Team are supporting schools in developing greater flexibility within the schools' workforce, which will support personalised learning. The infrastructure is developing to support one of the biggest changes to our education system since the 1870s.

What do other people say about personalising learning?

The DfES (2004b) leaflet, 'A National Conversation about Personalised Learning', defines PL in terms of five principles:

- for children and young people, clear learning pathways through the education system and the motivation to become independent, e-literate, fulfilled, life-long learners;
- for schools, a professional ethos that accepts that every child comes to the classroom with a different knowledge base and skills set and that there should be the determination for every young person's needs to be assessed and their talents developed through diverse teaching strategies;
- for school governors, promoting high standards of educational achievement and wellbeing for every pupil, ensuring that all aspects of organising and running the school work together to get the best for all pupils;
- for the DfES and local authorities, a responsibility to create the conditions in which teachers and schools have the flexibility and capability to personalise the learning experience of all their pupils; combined with a system of intelligent accountability so that central intervention is in inverse proportion to success; and
- for the system as a whole, the shared goals of high quality and high equity.

The DfES leaflet then sets out the components of personalised learning as follows:

- assessment for learning, and the use of evidence and dialogue to identify every pupil's learning needs;
- effective teaching and learning strategies that develop the competence and confidence of every learner by actively engaging and stretching them;
- curriculum entitlement and choice that delivers breadth of study, personal relevance and flexible learning pathways through the system;
- school organisation, with school leaders and teachers thinking creatively about how to support high-quality teaching and learning; and
- strong partnership beyond the school to drive forward progress in the class-room, to remove barriers to learning and to support pupil wellbeing.

Charles Leadbeater, a senior research associate with the independent think tank Demos and adviser to the Downing Street Policy Unit, has been engaged in work with the DfES Innovations Unit, the National College for School Leadership and Demos on personalisation. He wrote a pamphlet for this group entitled 'Learning about Personalisation: how can we put the learner at the heart of the education system?'. In it he talks about young people as having:

- choice in what they learn;
- choice in how they learn; and
- choice in how they are assessed.

He states that personalisation isn't about doing anything radically different: it's about doing what you're supposed to be doing better. He encourages teachers and schools to think radically about what educational institutions could be like and to spread the capability to take action, by gathering evidence about what works.

David Hopkins, then the head of the DfES Standards and Effectiveness Unit, said we have the potential to bring about a major and dramatic shift in the education system.

> It's building schooling around the needs and aptitudes of individual pupils, shaping teaching around the way different youngsters learn. It's also making sure that the talent of each pupil is supported and encouraged and about personalising the school experience to enable pupils to focus on their learning.

He reminds us that personalisation is not about shying away from the standards agenda. Indeed, he says it should have a standards focus. He defined personalised learning as:

- defining teaching, curriculum and school organisation to address the needs of the individual pupil;
- a learning offer to all children that extends beyond the school context into the local community and beyond;
- an approach to teaching and learning that focuses on an individual's potential and learning skills;
- a system that recognises and supports the needs of the whole child;
- a system that removes barriers to learning early on; and
- a system that is more accessible and open to customisation.

He says that the agenda is around action and experimentation.

David Hargreaves has been at the forefront of discussions and research about learning and how it can be made more efficient and effective for our learners in schools. His work has contributed much to our growing understanding of what personalised learning should look like. He says that personalising learning will:

- reinforce some current practices in schools and classrooms;
- demand modifications to some current practices; and
- entail creating some new practices.

He considers PL in terms of nine interconnected gateways:

1 curriculum
2 advice and guidance
3 assessment for learning
4 learning how to learn
5 the new technologies
6 workforce development
7 mentoring
8 school design and organisation
9 student voice

He challenges schools to create networks of innovation, starting from the different gateways according to the needs and preferences of individual networks, but then to bring the outcomes of the different networks together to produce an overall, coherent version of personalisation as a well of resources from which everyone can draw.

Much of the current literature, particularly that from the DfES, talks about *personalised* learning as if it were something that can be done, finished and ticked off as completed, but I have deliberately used the phrase *personalising learning*, because I see the process as a never-ending journey of discovery about what works for each individual. There should never be an end to this journey, because we should always be learning for ourselves about how to improve, and there will always be the challenge of new learners at our school gates.

So what's the solution to providing PL?

The bad news is that there is no one-size-fits-all solution to PL. The very essence of it is that learning should be different for every learner. Learning shouldn't be about squeezing children through the 'sausage-factory' curriculum so that they all come out the other end with a set level. It should reflect their needs, their wants, their dreams, their developing abilities and skills, and develop their talents and excite them with new interests.

If you want to develop PL within your primary school, this book will provide you with some checklists of questions to ask yourselves, some step-by-step guidance and frameworks that you can adapt to your needs. But it will not provide the answer to what PL will look like for *your* pupils in *your* school. That is for you to determine, in close collaboration with your staff, parents, governors and, most importantly, your pupils.

It is often said that there is nothing new in the world of education, and if you wait long enough trends will come round again. I believe that is the case for PL. Many of the 'components' considered in this book have been out there in the educational field and have been tried in many schools, by many teachers and are backed up by theory based on extensive research. There are no new magic techniques in this book: it is just a holistic approach that is based on years of trying to develop effective practice. The only secret about the successful implementation of personalising learning is to ensure that it is a whole-school approach to putting the learning needs of every individual child first, so that a solution can be found to empower learners to manage their own learning.

There are, of course, going to be implications for teachers, for how schools are led and managed, for how learning is organised and how assessment is conducted and so forth. There are lots of issues to be considered before you embark on PL in your school, but don't let that put you off. You need to remember that there is probably much practice within your institution already that could be part of your solution to personalising learning.

So why bother?

There is nothing so unequal as the equal treatment of unequals.

– BLANCHARD, 1994

Although Blanchard was writing about leadership, what he says also rings true about our current education system. Children enter the system bringing with them their own unique set of abilities. They all come from very different backgrounds and pre-school learning experiences, and yet we expect them to operate in a system that does not recognise and celebrate their individuality.

PL is a way of not only recognising that individuality but a way of celebrating it and encouraging children to use their individual skills and talents to improve what they can be. In our school, we found the benefits of working towards personalising learning were that:

- the children were motivated to learn;
- incidents of bad behaviour were minimal because the children were operating in a system that they did not need to 'kick' against;
- the staff were motivated and gave 110 per cent;
- the parents were supportive of what was happening and became engaged in learning about learning themselves;
- the school developed a good reputation for caring for the individual and being inclusive;
- lots of other schools wanted to visit to look at what we did and how we managed it; and
- standards were good (and improving).

So where do you begin?

Where you begin, of course, depends on where you are starting from! PL is going to be different in every institution that adopts it, because it needs to be tailor-made to fit the pupils and the community that you serve.

I hope that there are some ideas here that you will be able to trial, adapt as necessary to fit your needs and make your own practice. The key is to have a go and see what happens.

CHAPTER 2

What Do We Already Know About Learning?

The mind and brain

The mind or the brain is at the heart of all learning. When we talk to children about learning, we always remind them to switch their brains on, but actually we need them to engage their minds too. The mind is the bigger concept encompassing all of our personality. Psychology gives us many insights into its operation, as does educational research. From neuroscience we are finally beginning to see inside the brain and marvel at the electrical and chemical impulses that make it tick. But we are only just beginning to understand how mind and brain really work.

From psychology we are gaining new insights about the nature of intelligence, the importance of self-esteem and the ways in which different environments, and our emotional reaction to them, can affect us. A positive attitude and the power of the human will can make all the difference to learning (or not).

From neuroscience we are finding out more about the structure of the brain. Scientists have been able to see what is happening when we are undertaking various activities and have learned more about what occurs when we are under stress and begin to see what is going on when we remember (or forget) things. Whereas we once thought of the brain in terms of having two halves or three parts, we now realise that this is far too simplistic a view of this powerful learning organ, but it nevertheless provides us with some simple science to underpin our understanding of learning and what hinders and helps the process.

We know that the brain is divided into three parts: the *reptilian brain*, the *limbic system* and the *neocortex*. Each is responsible for different functions. The reptilian brain governs our most basic survival instincts; for example, our breathing, circulation and so on. The limbic system is responsible for processing emotions and dealing with the input from the senses and with our long-term memory (you can see why there is a strong connection between our emotions and long-term memory and why smell is such a powerful memory booster). The neocortex deals with our higher-order thinking and reasoning. All three parts of the brain work together to ensure prime function, but, if one or more of these parts is not satisfied by its stimulation through the environment, then learning opportunities and potential will be diminished.

It becomes obvious, then, why we need to consider our most basic needs in order to ensure that learning takes place. If we are, say, cold, tired, hungry or upset, then our brain is unable to engage its high-order functions of learning and thinking. We need to keep ourselves comfortable in terms of environment and emotional state to enable ourselves to be open to learning.

The brain can also be thought about in terms of its two hemispheres – left and right. We have known for a very long time that the left side controls the right-hand side of our bodies and vice versa. It is now thought that the left-hand side of the brain specialises in language, logic and number concepts, working in a very logical and sequential way. The right side specialises in nonverbal and intuitive thinking, dealing with imagination and intuition. The two hemispheres are joined together by the *corpus callosum*, which allows communication between the two sides. The most effective thinking and learning takes place when both sides of the brain are working together. This means that we need to consider activities to ensure that pupils stimulate both sides of the brain. For example, putting learning to music – singing times tables – combining numbers with rhyme and rhythm.

The environment

The environment has a huge impact on learning, in terms of the physical environment, but, more importantly, the emotional environment needs to be 'right' in order for learning to take place. Unless the relationship between learner and learning facilitator is characterised by trust and mutual respect, the learning process will be impacted upon in a negative way.

The learner must be physically comfortable in their environment for learning opportunities to be maximised – so the space for learning, the temperature, levels of lighting, availability of fresh air, seating arrangements, provision of drinking water and healthy snacks must all be considered. Physical discomfort can minimise learning.

Gender differences

We now know what educationalists have always suspected: that the brains of boys and girls are slightly different. The corpus callosum has been found to be thicker, therefore more effective, in female brains. This means that the male has a tendency to use only one hemisphere at any one time, making him focused and dogmatic. The male brain has a larger area for visual/spatial processing, making males much better at such things as construction activities, playing football and reading maps. The female brain has a much lower level of testosterone, making females more cooperative and compliant. The male brain has a lower level of serotonin, and this is associated with poor behavioural control and acting without thinking. It makes males greater risk takers. The female brain has a higher level of dopamine, enabling her to pay attention and maintain effort for longer periods than the male.

These are, of course, broad findings that highlight the stereotypes of male and female behaviour, and there is far more that is similar than is different. It can be dangerous to exaggerate and stereotype differences, and there will, of course, be a wide range of observable behaviours in both sexes. But these perceived gender differences provide some explanation for the differences seen in learning behaviours exhibited by boys and girls in classrooms and needs to be part of your observation of individual learners and your response in facilitating learning.

Learning cycles

Every single one of us is unique, and therefore we each have our own way of looking at, interacting with and learning from the world in which we live. There are many and varied learning-style profiles that are available, but by the very act of labelling a child with a particular learning-style profile you are undermining your quest for personalising learning. It is not about labelling a child: it is about knowing the child as an individual, supporting them in knowing themselves as a learner and providing a rich and varied learning environment to aid and support their learning.

Many neuroscientists agree that our performance as learners is dramatically influenced by our biological rhythms. These rhythms are regulated by the limbic system in our brains but are influenced by our genes, the solar and lunar cycles and other environmental factors.

We each have our own unique learning cycle: some of us are morning people, for instance, and others prefer to burn the midnight oil; some of us can concentrate for long periods of time, and others need to work in short, sharp bursts. It is no different for the children in our schools and we need to observe and discuss with the children the time when they feel they do their best learning.

We need to consider, when planning our learning activities, that we are providing opportunities for children to engage in the full range of learning activities at different times of the day so it is not all 'work' in the morning and all 'play' in the afternoon.

Learning to learn

If we think about learning in terms of the attitudes and skills needed to be an effective lifelong learner rather than the specific knowledge content of what we learn, then learning skills can be practised and developed over time. 'Learning is learnable' (Lucas, 2001).

Guy Claxton (1999) talked about the three Rs of learning: *resilience, resourceful-ness* and *reflectiveness*. Bill Lucas (2001) took this work further and added another two Rs: *remembering* and *responsiveness*. If we want to help our pupils develop as effective lifelong learners, we need to be providing activities and learning experiences that will help them develop and strengthen these 'learnacy' (Claxton) skills.

1 Resilience

Resilience is about sticking at something when it becomes tough – having an inner determination to succeed. In order to be encouraged to develop resilience, children need to experience the thrill of success. Once that feeling is embedded in their brain, they will want to experience it again and again. Lucas (2001) talks about resilience in terms of four main areas:

- how you persist;
- being an adventurer;
- dealing with difficulties; and
- dealing with confusion.

Children will need encouragement to develop all four of these areas. Very young children have very short concentration spans, usually, and they will need to be provided with an environment that stimulates and engages them if they are to be encouraged to develop their concentration for longer periods. Feedback from a learning facilitator on how long children have worked at an activity will enable them to see that they are developing this skill. Praise and encouragement will reinforce this and encourage them to stick at things for a longer period in the future.

Children are natural adventurers, riddled with curiosity about their world. We need to harness this and provide lots of opportunities for them to have adventures. This will mean not planning the learning activities too tightly.

How children deal with difficulties in their learning can provide a clear guide as to how successful they will be as a learner. If they stop at the first sign of a problem, then they will never experience success and will never be motivated to put themselves through the agony of failure again. If they learn how to have a go and try things out or where to go for support or help and are willing to get things wrong sometimes, then they will have a much more positive approach to learning and are more likely to succeed. So the learning facilitator will need to be 'around' to provide support when the going gets tough, but must never be tempted to complete the learning for the child. Maybe a prompt or question will be all that it takes to put them back on track. Maybe it will take some encouragement and support. Whatever it is, the learning facilitator will need to know when to spot that a child has become 'stuck' because of a difficulty – this can be done only through close observation, because, if you wait for the child to come to you or show frustration by leaving an activity, then it is too late. If you have more than one adult in a classroom, you could share the observation duties – one adult always being an observer of learners at work. They can then be asked to provide feedback on their observations during the plenary session.

Handling confusion is an important part of the learning journey. It is not a case of plotting your route and marching confidently from your starting point to your intended destination. The path is littered with all sorts of obstacles. Sometimes when we are learning, 'stuff' happens that we weren't expecting. It is how we encourage young learners to handle this confusion that will support them in becoming effective and efficient lifelong learners. Sometimes, as learners, we just need time for the 'penny to drop', and knowing when to leave something and give ourselves time to think is a real lifelong-learning skill. Children will know that it is all right to leave something and come back to it later only if we make room for that to happen and model it for them sometimes. I am sure that we have all experienced the child who is forever out of their seat, sharpening their pencil, looking for a rubber, going to the toilet for the third time in ten minutes – maybe they just need some thinking time.

We need to recognise what happens when we are learning something new as adults, that it doesn't always go smoothly and we will all have our own ways of finding our way through something – developing our resilience. If it is all right for adults to do this, then it should be all right for our children as learners to find their own way through too. As adults who are learning facilitators, we will need to be forever challenging our assumptions about the learning process and helping our children see that it is a complicated and messy business, but that they will get better at it with time and practice and lots of support.

2 Resourcefulness

Resourcefulness is all about the learner developing their own approach to their learning – finding out what works best for them. It is about learning from and with others, about learning in different ways and being flexible as a learner. The resourceful learner will know how their brain and mind works; they will understand their own learning environment and how to maximise their efficiency as a learner within that environment. They will have a range of approaches to learning and will be able to communicate their learning in a variety of different ways and they will be able to use a range of learning tools, including ICT (information and communications technology), to great effect.

It will be our role as learning facilitators to encourage resourcefulness in the learners by having a well-resourced learning environment, with a wide range of learning tools available (and working). We will need to provide a wide range of open-ended learning activities so that the children can be flexible in how they meet the learning objective. Sometimes it will be about leaving the learning outcome open, so that the children can choose whether they write about it, dance about it, paint about it or make a poster about it; they can reflect their learning in a way that is meaningful to them. We will need to create opportunities for children to work together and learn from each other. I am not talking about administrative grouping of children for organisational purposes, but real group work that supports the children in developing the skills needed to work as effective members of a team.

3 Reflectiveness

One major criticism of our classrooms today is that they are always very busy places – in terms of content coverage and so forth. Children are always expected to provide an immediate response to an instruction to complete a task or provide an answer to a question. When do they get time to stop and think? If they are to become skilled learners, they need to develop reflectiveness. They need time to stop and think, look back over their learning, reflect on the processes they have experienced and consider which were effective for them and why. Do you provide thinking time for your learners?

You will need to consider your activities over a day/week/half-term period, to ensure that you are building in a balance of busy times and reflection times. We don't always have to have hands-on learning, being constantly busy doing things; sometimes we need to make time for 'brains-on' learning, when we can do some deep thinking instead of doing.

4 Remembering

Memory is an important part of being an effective learner. Children can be helped to maximise their memory. They can be 'taught' simple techniques that will help them recall things more easily. Mnemonics, for example, can be used to great effect. Everyone will remember being taught 'Every Good Boy Deserves Favour' to aid our memory of the notes on the stave in music, or 'Richard Of York Gained Battle In Vain' to remember the colours of the rainbow. There are many examples of mnemonics that can be used, or why not get the children to make up their own?

Practise, repetition and review works to help improve memory. If this is done in short bursts and repeated several times it will be most effective. Using role play, drama, hot-seating and visualisation techniques can also be taught and used effectively to retain things in the memory. These techniques work because the children are actively involved in their learning and they often involve humour and other emotions that are proven to be a key factor to memory. When you think back to your own school days, what are the most powerful memories for you? For me, it was times when I was engaged in exciting activities such as the school play or on a visit to an exciting or different place. Or it was times when I experienced extreme emotion – being in trouble for not knowing my nine-times table and having to stand in front of the blackboard all day, where it was written, supposedly to help me remember it. (I didn't actually learn my nine-times table until I was nineteen, at college, when a lecturer showed me that all the answers added up to nine and that the tens ascended while the units descended.) We need to use emotion (in a positive way) as an aid to memory.

Another way to support committing things to memory is to use the powerful technique of mind mapping or concept mapping. This is a simple skill that can be taught at an early age – we introduced it from Year 1 – and children can use it as an aid for planning, review and revision. A good guide to the use of mind maps as a learning tool is *Mapwise* (Caviglioli and Harris, 2000).

5 Responsiveness

Responsiveness is about how we react to change and manage our feelings about the process. To be an effective learner, it is essential that you can learn to do things differently and stay positive about your learning, particularly when things go wrong. This is a huge step for us to expect our primary-aged children to cope with, and it goes back again to the climate for learning that we create and maintain in our schools and classrooms. If, as adult learners, we can model a positive approach to change, to new learning and to new situations, and to making mistakes or getting things wrong, then it is more likely that our pupils will develop this positive outlook too.

In order to develop our children as lifelong learners, we should be helping them develop their 'learnacy' skills in the five Rs, so that they begin to understand how learning works for them.

Learning styles

Our learning style can be defined as the individual way in which we interact with our environment, how we take in information most easily and how we process that information. Our learning style is made up of cognitive, biological and psychological factors, including whether we like to work alone or with others; our preferred time of day for working; our requirements for food and drink; our preferences for our ideal working environment in terms of comfort, heat and light; our intelligence profile (in terms not of IQ but of the multiple-intelligences work of Dr Howard Gardner of Harvard University, of whom more shortly) and the way our brain works, which can be dependent on our gender. Theory tells us that learning is optimised when our learning style is catered for – but how do we begin to consider meeting individual learning styles when the permutations of the above factors are incalculable?

The answer is that as adults we are not responsible for meeting the individual learning styles of our pupils, but, rather, it is the learners' responsibility to think about and make decisions about the way that they learn best and to optimise learning opportunities for themselves. The learners need to know themselves as learners and to develop strategies that work for them. Our responsibility as learning facilitators is to ensure that our children are given the time and opportunity to do this thinking and are provided with the background knowledge to support their decision making and the language to describe their learning needs to others.

Motivation

For most of us as adults, we would be motivated by something that we have an interest in, something that sparks our imagination or curiosity and where learning it would make an impact on us, in terms of either our ability to impress others with our skills or knowledge, or whether the skill or knowledge had obvious future uses. Shouldn't we be offering learning experiences for our pupils that would stimulate the same levels of motivation and engagement?

Memory and recall

This ties in very closely with remembering in the five-Rs section earlier. Jenson in *Brain-Based Learning* (2000) shows how memories are formed. He says that:

- we think, feel, move and experience life (sensory stimulation).
- all experiences are registered in the brain.
- they are prioritised by value, meaning and usefulness by brain structures and processes.
- many individual neurons are activated.
- neurons transmit information to other neurons via electrical and chemical reactions; and

- these connections are strengthened by repetition, rest and emotions; lasting memories are formed.

Techniques can then be used to improve memory and recall:

- use **storytelling** and **visualisations** in your direct teaching;
- encourage pupils to look for **patterns** and **connections** with prior learning;
- make it memorable – use **humour** or **emotion** to help children remember;
- use acrostics and other **mnemonic techniques**;
- use large, colourful **learning posters** that the children have helped to create;
- present learning in **short bursts** (we remember beginnings and endings of presentations and lose bits from the middle, so, if you break learning into smaller, bite-sized chunks, you create more beginnings and endings);
- **review** learning frequently;
- use **mind maps**; and
- provide time for **thinking** and **reflecting**.

Multiple intelligences

Over the twentieth century there was a widespread view that our ability to learn depended on how 'intelligent' we are. IQ was thought to be a fixed limit on an individual's capacity to learn. Indeed, this was the basis of selection by the eleven-plus examination – only those clever enough could go to grammar school and continue to be effective learners. Thinking about children in terms of how intelligent they are can be a dangerous mindset for teachers to have, as we all know the theories around teacher expectation and self-fulfilling prophecies.

This theory was overthrown by Howard Gardner of Harvard, who developed a theory of multiple intelligences, comprising at least seven types of intelligence, which were not fixed but were capable of development and expansion. The theory of multiple intelligences shows us, as teachers, that intelligence can be expandable and is much more inclusive. Gardner wanted us to stop asking the question, 'How intelligent is this child?' and start asking the question, 'How is this child intelligent?'. Gardner's (1984) original seven intelligences were:

- **linguistic intelligence:** relating to language and expression through words written or spoken;
- **logical-mathematical intelligence:** relating to mathematical and scientific approaches, manipulation of numbers and abstract symbols, logical structured approach to problem solving;
- **visual-spatial intelligence:** relating to visualisation and manipulation of images, construction of models, understanding of spatial relationships;
- **bodily kinaesthetic intelligence:** relating to movement and use of the body in a controlled way;
- **musical intelligence:** relating to a sensitivity to music, sound and rhythm;
- **interpersonal intelligence:** relating to a sensitivity towards other people, understanding and predicting their responses, and communicating well; and
- **intrapersonal intelligence:** relating to a sense of self and awareness of own feelings, strengths and areas for development.

He then went on to add an eighth: *naturalistic intelligence*, relating to the natural world, to awareness of patterns and meaning in nature, to taking a keen interest in your environment.

'Each of us has all of them,' said Gardner, 'but in different measure and combined in different ways.'

Multiple intelligence, as a theory of intelligence, is contested and has the potential to be misused in our classrooms. Teachers took Gardner's theory to mean that they should become more aware of the differing profiles of their pupils and expand their range of teaching strategies accordingly, in order to try to meet individual learning needs. In terms of PL, they have missed the point. They should still observe pupils in terms of the types of intelligence that they display, but they need to take it one stage further and provide feedback to the pupils about what they observe and then ask the pupils what they intend to do with the information. We should be using these theories to underpin the pupils' developing understanding of themselves as independent learners, not as an end in themselves.

Music

As summarised by Webb and Webb (1990), music can have a huge impact on the mind and body. It can:

- increase muscular energy;
- increase molecular energy;
- influence heartbeat;
- alter metabolism;
- reduce pain and stress;
- speed healing and recovery in surgery patients;
- relieve fatigue;
- aid in the release of emotions; and
- stimulate creativity, sensitivity and thinking.

Steven Halpern (1985; and at www.musica.uci.edu) claims that the use of music in the curriculum can aid maths, reading and science learning. He goes on to say that the learning benefits attributed to music are:

- relaxation and stress reduction (stress inhibits learning);
- the fostering of creativity through brainwave activation;
- the stimulation of imagination and thinking;
- the stimulation of motor skills, speaking and vocabulary;
- a reduction in discipline problems;
- the focusing and alignment of group energy; and
- as a vehicle for conscious and subconscious information transmission.

While music undoubtedly affects our mood and our emotions, its direct impact on learning and performance is contested. But music can have its place in personalising-learning classrooms – some children will find that certain types of music help them to concentrate (while for others it will be an irritant) and music can certainly be used to create atmosphere or set the ethos within the classroom.

Schemas

Piaget says (Piaget and Inhelder, 1969, p.4) a 'scheme' or 'schema' is 'the structure or organisation of actions as they are transferred or generalised by repetition in similar or analogous circumstances.' Chris Athey (1981) undertook research into schemas, which she defined as 'a pattern of repeated behaviour into which experiences are assimilated and are gradually co-ordinated'(p. 37). Athey suggests that children work on various schemas in their development. Close observation of children may reveal that a child may be paying attention to a predominant schema at a certain time. Athey suggests that suitable experiences and provision should be matched to the pattern of behaviour (schema) in order to extend the child's learning. A schema cannot be taught but stems from the intrinsic motivation of the child. This must be facilitated by provision and supported by adults as they give children the freedom to choose their materials. A workshop approach would be beneficial to achieve this. The most common schemas are:

- **transporting:** moving objects from one place to another;
- **positioning:** placing objects, often seen in painting and drawings;
- **orientation:** turning objects or self upside down;
- **enclosure:** creating a structure with construction materials, e.g. blocks; also seen as circles or lines around elements in paintings;
- **enveloping:** covering objects or self with varying materials, e.g. dressing up;
- **diagonality:** drawings may show diagonal lines, e.g. outdoors – building slides, ramps, etc.;
- **dab:** a graphic scheme, seen in paintings to represent eyes or other small circular items;
- **horizontality/verticality:** often body actions, e.g. stepping up and down or lying flat, later used graphically to form crosses or grids;
- **transforming:** showing interest in how materials can change, e.g. shape, colour, consistency;
- **radial:** graphic representations, e.g. eyelashes, spiders, suns;
- **rotation:** an interest in things that turn, e.g. knobs, taps, keys; may roll own body and body parts;
- **connection:** frequently seen at the woodwork bench, craft or collage table; disconnecting is part of this schema, as in taking a construction apart;
- **semicirculatory:** graphically represented as eyebrows, smiles, parts of letters of the alphabet;
- **ordering:** placing objects in line or painting or drawing with ordered lines, gluing with scraps;
- **correspondence:** placing objects into segmented containers, e.g. pieces of dough into an egg box;
- **functional dependency:** the dependency of one function on another, e.g. the oven needs to be turned on in order to bake the cake; and
- **trajectory:** straight line, either up and down or across, seen in the use of body parts, e.g. throwing, kicking and in drawing or painting lines.

You can use the language of schemas to describe observed learning behaviours and you can make provision accordingly in order to move the children on in their learning.

Visual, auditory, kinaesthetic

We have, of course, five senses and they can all be used to help us learn. Most people, naturally, will have a dominant sense or one they favour or have more highly developed than the others. The three most common senses considered in terms of learning in classrooms are referred to as VAK: visual, auditory, kinaesthetic. VAK is not, as it is sometimes referred to, a learning style. It is a means of inputting data into our brains and is, as such, not fixed and can change with the child's age, stage of development or mood.

Essentially, visual learners learn from what they see, auditory learners learn from what they hear and kinaesthetic learners learn from movement and what they touch. We all learn through all three methods, but each of us will have a preferred one for inputting data into our brains. This will obviously have an impact in the classroom and, if you undertake observations of children, you will find it to be significant.

If we are going to personalise learning, we should be considering these elements when planning our curriculum delivery. Are our inputs (our teaching) always delivered through the same medium? If we plan some of our week's programme with a variety of inputs, we will be beginning to address the individual learning needs of the children.

While the VAK approach is based on the senses most easily used in the classroom, we should not underestimate the power of the other two senses – taste and smell. Our olfactory (smell) and gustatory (taste) senses can also be used to help fix learning. Some of my staff were convinced about the efficacy of using aromatherapy oils in burners within their classrooms. Lavender oil was particularly popular on windy days in helping calm the children. Citrus oil was found to be efficacious when it came to SATs time, stimulating thinking.

CHAPTER 3

Whole-School Systems

I think she's taking this whole 'Brain Gym' thing just too far!

Assessment for learning

You will need to adopt a system of assessment that complements your approach to personalising learning. There has been some powerful research into the impact of formative assessment on raising achievement (Black and Wiliam, 1998; Clarke, 2001). It provides a sound basis for providing meaningful feedback to pupils in order to support them in improving their performance, which in turn will impact on standards of attainment.

Clarke provides an excellent framework, starting with planning, sharing learning intentions with pupils, pupils' self-evaluation, feedback and target setting, underpinned by the most vital aspect of her work, raising children's self-esteem.

Clarke's focus marking strategy will enable you to ensure that every pupil receives the same amount of feedback, regardless of their ability. She says that you should always mark to the learning objective, highlighting three places where the child has met the success criteria and one place where they could make some improvement.

Behaviour management

In order to support PL, you will want to put into place a positive behaviour-management system that supports the development of self-discipline in the pupils.

The trick is to catch the children doing things well, or doing the right thing and praise them for it. Celebrate good behaviour during plenary sessions and at assembly time, just as you would celebrate good work. If it is your school policy to award stickers and certificates, then these should be awarded for good behaviour just as they would be awarded for good work.

Wherever possible, ignore low-level bad behaviour so that the child learns that they will receive no attention for disrupting learning. Do not even make eye contact with the child. Instead, praise the good behaviour of the children sitting around them. Give the badly behaved child eye contact and praise only when they do the slightest thing right.

If you have to intervene because the behaviour could be harmful to the child or others around them, do it quietly and sensitively, to the child alone, not publicly in front of the whole class. Discussions can be held about 'what would you do if…' scenarios during circle time to assist the children in developing their sense of right and wrong and airing their feelings about making the right decisions.

Brain Gym®

Brain Gym® involves simple movements, which, it is claimed, have the effect of integrating the left and right brain hemispheres, making learning more effective. It can be used to improve almost any skill, whether mental or physical, and to bring emotional and physical wellbeing into balance.

Brain Gym® activities help form a bridge between the two sides of the brain and help children to stimulate the whole brain to be ready for learning. You can use the exercises as part of your daily teaching programme to reinvigorate children if they are beginning to flag or as a bridge between activities. It helps to focus children's attention and reoxygenate the brain. (You can use them with adults too.)

Circle time/bubble time

Children need to feel that their voices can be heard. You need to have systems in place in your school to help children learn to manage difficult situations, handle conflict and talk about their feelings. Jenny Mosley's (1998) circle time and bubble time provide a whole-school framework to enable these discussions to take place.

Your staff will need to plan systematically for circle time and ensure that every child is given the opportunity to contribute to the discussions. Circle time can play an important part in your discussions about social and moral issues and often helps the children work through difficulties that they are experiencing at home, with the support of their peers.

Bubble time is used for individual pupils who need to have some one-to-one time with an adult (of their choice) to discuss issues that are causing them concern or distress. Children can either ask discreetly for this time or there can be an agreed signalling procedure. This will need to be discussed and agreed with the children first.

Collaborative group reading

In many schools children are grouped for reading based on their ability. I have never understood this practice. I have always understood one of the rationales for grouping children together is that they have an opportunity to learn from each other. If children are grouped by ability, the learning of some, particularly those at the lower end of the perceived ability range, may be restricted.

Mixed-ability reading groups facilitate support for all readers by providing role models of what reading involves. All children can be encouraged during collaborative group reading sessions to discuss the reading strategies that they employ. For some, this will be looking at the pictures for clues; others will be using their phonic knowledge and yet others will use the whole-word approach. By explaining their strategies to others they will be 'cementing' them in their own minds, but they may also hear about other strategies that they can employ in order to develop further their reading skills.

If you want to adopt this approach to the teaching of reading, the class should be split into five mixed-ability, collaborative reading groups (one for each day of the week). Each day an adult should work with the focus group, while the other four groups get on with reading activities. These could include:

- continuing to read;
- working on character profiles;
- working on setting profiles;
- devising an alternative ending for the story;
- discussion on what has been read;
- drawing/painting/collage/making models of the story;
- designing a book cover;
- writing a blurb for the book;
- research about the author;
- research about the genre; and
- research about the subject.

The list of possible tasks is almost endless. The important thing to remember is that they should be collaborative by nature, where the children are working together and discussing their learning. The adult working with the focus group will need to work through the following group reading stages:

- Identify the learning objective for the session.
- Select a text that will support the objective.
- Encourage discussion before reading about the book. Do the children know what the story might be about, recognise the author, illustrator, genre, style? Do they know other, similar, books?
- Talk about what is going to happen in the group – whether the children will be reading aloud or silently, for instance, taking it in turns to read however many pages, expected to identify certain features of the text.
- Encourage the children to familiarise themselves with the text by flicking through. The adult should then begin reading (modelling), then the children can continue reading.

- Beginner readers – go through the book building up the story in discussion. Encourage the readers to identify known words, sounds and language patterns. The adult should read the complete text and discuss the story with the children. The book can be used again at another time to reinforce processes and further extend or consolidate learning and understanding.
- Non-fluent readers: encourage the readers to have a go at the text using phonological, word-recognition and/or contextual clues etc. Encourage readers to use aspects of the text to make sense of what they are reading, e.g. grammar, syntax, context. Discuss similarities with other stories/characters they know.
- Moderately fluent readers: encourage the flow of the text as it is read, intervening only to reinforce the learning objective. At selected points share and discuss what has been read. Encourage a short period of silent reading. Share and discuss what has been read silently, encouraging children to refer to text to justify their views and compare with other texts read.
- Confident, fluent readers: reading a long book split into chapters, children should read aloud for a short time, then read on silently. Adults should engage with individual readers to ensure they have an active attitude towards reading. Finally, share within the group their views and opinions on what has been read. Encourage them to read to a selected point.
- Follow-up activity: have a range of follow-up activities available for the children to choose from.

Golden Rules

The Golden Rules should be introduced to the children as early as possible in their school career. The rules should be discussed so that the children have a deep understanding of what they mean in their daily dealings with people. They should also understand that the Golden Rules don't apply only at school: they apply to life and should be used at all times in all places. You will need to provide their parents with a copy of the Golden Rules too so that they can display and use them at home.

Our Golden Rules were these:

We respect each other.
1 Do be gentle: don't hurt anyone.
2 Do be kind: don't hurt other people's feelings.
3 Do be honest: don't hide the truth.
4 Do look after property: don't waste or damage it.
5 Do listen well: don't interrupt.
6 Do work hard: don't waste your time or others' time.
Treat others as you would like to be treated.

Golden Time

Golden Time is closely linked to the Golden Rules and needs to be a set time during the week so that the whole school participates at the same time, thereby reducing possible disruption. All children have an entitlement to twenty minutes of Golden Time per week, provided that they have not broken the Golden Rules (remember, these apply everywhere, not just at school). Golden Time can be used for any purpose chosen by each child. The children can:

- work on a favourite activity;
- work in another classroom or area of the school;
- play a favourite game;
- spend time with a sibling in their classroom;
- visit the library or use the Internet for research; and
- job-shadow members of staff (headteacher, deputy headteacher, office staff, site staff).

The list can be endless, provided that the health-and-safety implications have been considered. If children break the Golden Rules, then they can have minutes removed from their entitlement of twenty. You should always try to keep these takeaway minutes to a minimum and children should have the right to earn them back, in order to learn forgiveness. The lost minutes can be earned back only from the person who withdrew them in the first place, so that the child will have to try to make amends for their misdeeds.

Homework

It is important that your homework policy supports and builds upon the approach to PL that you have adopted in your classrooms. If children have a growing level of choice in learning activities during school time, they should have the corresponding level of choice in their homework, too. Children can use their individual mind maps to provide some guidance into the areas of study for homework. We ensured that this element of individualised study at home was built into a homework policy that was shared with parents, too.

But there are still some 'basics' that need to be part of a homework schedule. The personalisation of this form of learning will be in the approaches that the children and their parents take to it. For example, some children will best learn their times tables by singing them or dancing to them, others by drawing grids and colouring in number patterns. Discussion will need to take place to ensure that the parents are aware of the variety of strategies that can be adopted to support their children's learning.

A copy of our homework schedule is included as Table 3.1 for your information. (IMPACT Maths is a scheme produced by BEAM that provides lots of interactive and exploratory maths activities that can be completed at home and calls for children and parents to learn and explore them together – more details can be found on the BEAM website: www.beam.co.uk.)

Key experiences

In order to enrich the curriculum, following discussion with the staff and governors, it was decided that we would generate a list of key experiences that each child should have an entitlement to, as part of our curriculum provision, on an annual basis. The list that we generated is reproduced here for your information:

- taking part in a 'public performance' on an annual basis;

	READING	LITERACY ACTIVITIES	MATHS	OTHER WORK
Nursery	Parents and children to read daily – 5–15 minutes	Talk about topic	Counting Colours Shapes	
Reception	Parents and children to read daily – 5–15 minutes	Talk about topic Sound books		
Year 1	Daily reading – 10–20 minutes	Spellings	IMPACT Maths See www.beam.co.uk	Topic research and independent study – ideas will be given on the topic information sheet at the beginning of each topic or the children will determine their own areas of interest for individual study
Year 2	Daily reading – 10–20 minutes	Spellings and sentences	IMPACT Maths Times tables 2, 5, 10	
Year 3	Daily reading – 15–30 minutes Reading diary	Spellings	Times tables 2, 3, 5, 10 IMPACT Maths	
Year 4	Daily reading 15–30 minutes Reading diary	Spellings	Times tables 2–6, 10–11 IMPACT Maths	
Year 5	Daily reading – 15–30 minutes Reading diary	Spellings	Times tables 2–12 IMPACT Maths	
Year 6	Daily reading 15–30 minutes Reading Diary	Spellings	Times tables 2–12 IMPACT Maths	

Table 3.1 Homework activity

- seeing a creative artist at work within the school, to include visits from such people as authors and storytellers;
- seeing people from the community, who visit the school to explain their work;
- activities outside school:
  - school journey;
  - day visits to galleries, museums, places of worship;
  - field work;
  - local history and further afield visits;
  - visits to such places as theatres, cinemas;
- using artefacts and primary sources;
- collecting data over a long period of time, e.g. weather, and processing it;
- taking part in sports activities, including borough events;
- making a positive contribution to the community, both school and wider, through such activities as participation in classroom discussions, school council and collections, for the wider community; and
- discussing contemporary issues.

Learning and teaching policy

You will need to have discussions with your staff (and possibly governors and parents) about the principles that will underpin the type of learning and teaching in your school. Here were ours – they formed the core of our learning and teaching policy.

Learning

1 Pupils are entitled to have access to a wide range of learning materials, resources and real-life experiences.
2 Pupils are able to select materials and space in which to work, as appropriate to the task in hand.
3 Pupils are encouraged to take responsibility for caring for, organising and conserving learning resources in the classroom and school environment.
4 Pupils are given responsibility for organising and evaluating their learning and managing their own time.
5 Both independent and cooperative work by pupils will be facilitated and encouraged.
6 Pupils should be encouraged to ask questions and to persevere.
7 Learning activities should be planned to enable progression and to allow children to experience success.
8 The atmosphere within the school should facilitate the development of good learning attitudes, which are appropriate in a variety of learning situations.
9 Pupils' specific individual interests should be valued and developed.
10 Pupils should understand that they, and the school, are parts of a wider community.

Teaching

Learning will be facilitated by the progressive acquisition of knowledge, skills and understanding and by:

1 using teaching techniques that make use of appropriate methods suiting the topic as well as the pupils' stage of development and preferred ways of learning;
2 lessons having clear aims and purposes, as indicated in our planning, which takes into account early-learning goals (ELGs), attainment targets and programmes of study within the National Curriculum;
3 teachers having high expectations of each pupil in all areas of their learning;
4 accentuating the positive in behaviour, work and attitude and by setting a good example;
5 children being involved in varying degrees with planning, organising and evaluating their own learning, e.g. they should receive regular feedback to help them progress through thoughtful marking and discussion;
6 ensuring that relationships are positive and promote pupil motivation by making pupils feel welcomed, cared for, secure and valued as individuals, by developing their self-esteem and confidence – we do this through building on strengths to promote success, regular meetings with children and parents and the use of formative feedback;

7 where appropriate, children being encouraged to engage in learning at home, which may be spellings, tables, reading activities or work that complements and extends the work done in lessons; we encourage parents to help children with their learning at home;

8 encouraging children to show concern for others and to value each person's individual contribution;

9 providing as many opportunities as possible for first-hand experience and investigative work;

10 flexible grouping strategies: children should have the opportunity to be taught in whole-class lessons, as part of a collaborative group, in pairs and individually;

11 teachers recognising that the learning process and the acquisition of skills is more important than the learning of content knowledge;

12 children having opportunities to create, express, enact, recount and communicate to others using a variety of media;

13 recognising the importance of equal opportunities, taking account of special needs, gender, race, creed and class;

14 having an approach that allows for differentiation in the curriculum, preferably by outcome, to support both the less and more able, as well as those with special needs, in a sensitive manner;

15 at all stages recognising and planning appropriate assessment and record-keeping systems that are used to guide future planning and ensure progression; and

16 use of the classroom and school environment to reflect current work themes.

Meditation

We introduced meditation sessions to Key Stage 2 classes, to help the children centre themselves before beginning work. These sessions were particularly successful following a playtime or lunchtime break or if the weather had 'stirred them up'.

An adult uses music to create a positive, relaxed atmosphere and takes the children and other adults through the meditation exercises. The classes would have discussed why meditation is important and the benefits of doing it, and the children would have a firm grasp about its positive impact on their ability to learn.

Resources

You will need to consider how you spend your money on resources that will support PL in your school. We made the decision to purchase resources that could be used in a variety of ways to support learning rather than subject-specific printed schemes, which are extremely expensive and have restricted use in terms of securing PL. We bought:

- individual whiteboards and markers;
- digital cameras;
- video cameras;
- paper strimmers;
- comb-binding equipment;
- laminators;
- a large amount of consumable stock – different types and sizes and colours of paper, card and so forth for book making and display;

- resources for topics (these were mainly artefacts that were stored in topic-specific boxes and added to over the years);
- books for class and whole-school libraries;
- film, video, pictures and slides for topics;
- Internet access in all areas of the school; and
- laptop computers.

Staff and pupils need to be trained to use the equipment safely and creatively.

Some schools that do not use published schemes seem to spend just as much money and a lot of teacher time in producing endless worksheets for the pupils to complete. You need to decide if you think that this is an effective way of facilitating learning.

Worksheets do have their place, but they should be worksheets that aid the children in their learning, not just worksheets for the sake of keeping a group busy or for assessment purposes – seeing if children can do what you have just taught them to do.

Wherever possible, learning should be kept 'real', based on life experiences, providing opportunities for children to work collaboratively on problem-solving and decision-making activities. Children should be given the choice of how they represent their learning for others – this could take the form of, among other things, a learning poster, a dance, a drama, a poem or a story. The quality of the learning should be the focus, not the quantity of workbooks completed.

School council

In order to give the pupils a voice and engage them in the management and leadership activities of the school, you can establish a school council. Pupils should be democratically elected by their peers and should represent the views of their classmates during debates in council meetings on school issues. They should play an important part in liaising with their classmates and feeding back on the outcomes of the council's discussions. Some school councils even have responsibility for a small budget that they can utilise to support any decisions they make.

If pupils are going to use their experience as a school council representative as a real-life learning experience, then they will need to understand the formalities of running a meeting, such as:

- the role of the chair and speaking through the chair,
- the role of the scribe or minute taker; and
- the importance of recording discussions and minuting action points.

These will need to be explained to the council at the beginning of each academic year or as new councillors take up their seats, and will need to be modelled for them at every meeting. As the children gain experience and confidence, they can take over the roles of chair and minute taker for the group.

I have worked with some very successful and influential school councils. They have felt enabled to call 'expert witnesses' to the council meetings – for example, a site manager when grounds development was being discussed. One council I worked with even invited the local mayor to attend one of its meetings when it was discussing the impact of dog fouling in the local park – as a consequence, waste bins were provided by the council for the use of dog owners.

School council can also be served by class councils, where elected representatives for each class would convene regular meetings, usually before the school council meeting, to discuss issues that affect their class. If the class decides that the issue is relevant or important enough to be taken forward to the school council, then the matter would be passed on to its school council representatives.

Solution-focused approach

The solution-focused approach is a system for problem solving and decision making, adapted from the world of psychology. Its aim is to support individuals in resolving issues for themselves, with the support of another should they require it, which is empowering and enabling.

Pupils (and adults) should be encouraged to face issues or problems that are causing them concern, think about their preferred outcome and come up with at least two potential solutions. They can then seek out someone with whom to discuss their issue and potential solutions. During the discussion, other solutions may become apparent. The choice of solution is left to the owner of the problem and they need to understand that any course of action taken will have consequences and they must be prepared to deal with those outcomes.

Study buddies or learning partners

The idea of study buddies is based on the work of Geoff Hannan (2001). From his research into effective grouping for learning, he says that children should have the opportunity to work in a variety of pairings – you should plan for one-third to be in friendship pairings, one-third to be in single-gender non-friendship pairings and one-third to be in mixed-gender pairings. This should take the form of a rolling programme so that, during the time span of half a term, all pupils will have worked in a structured way with every other pupil in the class.

If you build into this programme of study buddies or learning partners, as a matter of course, a feedback system so that children are receiving – from a range of learning partners they have worked with – feedback on their own performance as a learning partner, each child will be building a very detailed picture of themselves as a learner within that context.

Wraparound care

In order to ensure continuity of provision, as a school we took the decision to employ our own staff to provide before- and after-school care in a breakfast club and after-school club. We also used our teaching assistants to provide continuity of care during the lunchtime period.

Children were being cared for and being encouraged to learn by the same people regardless of the context, e.g. the classroom, the playground, the dining hall or the pre- and post-school clubs.

Yoga

We used yoga in Key Stage 1 as a way of developing the children's physical being and to help to centre them for learning in the same way as we used meditation in Key Stage 2. An excellent resource for this is 'Yoga for Children' cards (Buckley, 2003).

CHAPTER 4

The Foundation Stage

Children enter their early years' setting as inquisitive, confident, lively, exciting and excitable learners and we seem to spend the next twelve or thirteen years 'knocking' that out of them so that they can learn what we need them to learn in order to pass exams or make the grade. Personalising learning will enable us to build on the natural learning abilities and aptitudes that the children bring with them at four or five years of age and will help them to develop as independent learners.

Let's start at the beginning

Get to know your learners

The only place to start if you are considering personalising learning is to get to know your learners, as individual people, as well as, as individual learners.

Build on existing experience

They come to you as vastly experienced learners who have been exploring their world for the four or five years that they have been a part of it. They have learned some of the most important skills that they will need in life before they come to you: they have learned how to communicate with others, how to be mobile and how to be self-sufficient in many things. We must never assume that the children come to us with no previous experience of learning or of being a learner. We must build on that experience and keep building upon it throughout their time in school if we want to personalise learning.

Who knows your learners best?

The people who know your learners best at this point are the people who have been watching them learn from birth: parents, grandparents or other carers, including childminders and au pairs and not forgetting any other workers in the pre-school setting who have been working with the child. You need to meet with these people in order to exchange this information so that you can begin to create your emerging picture of the child. You will need to decide who meets with these knowledge holders and how to encourage them to share what they know, honestly but in a sensitive and caring manner. You want these people to trust you.

How do you get parents to share their knowledge?

The best way to put people at ease is to meet with them on their own 'turf'. Many nurseries and schools now run a programme of home visits that usually take place just before the child enters the nursery or reception class, at the end of the term before the child enters or at the beginning of the term the child enters.

Many schools also work in partnership with local pre-school settings and arrange patterns of visits across the year or at least just before the children transfer. There is also a written communication from the pre-school setting to the nursery or school, which enables the transfer of important information and provides a summary of the child's profile. But, if you have the capacity, it is always a good idea to make a visit to the pre-school setting and talk to the staff about their understandings of the children.

How do you make initial contact with your parents?

If you are going to visit parents you already have an established relationship with, then it would be all right to cold-call them to arrange an appointment. If, however, you are initiating contact with a family you do not know, it is best not to cold-call because it will sound impersonal. It would be better to invite the parents into school for a visit (with their child if it was during the school day) or for an evening meeting. You can then talk to them about your school's policy on home visits and why they are so vital to the process of establishing a home–school partnership.

Never forget that parents are the first and best teachers of their children and you want to encourage them to continue their work as educators of their child and you want to become part of that partnership. It is not about the school assuming control and dictating to parents how they should bring up and educate their children.

At the end of the meeting, parents can be invited to sign up for a home visit on a day and at a time that is convenient to them.

top tip

It is a good idea to have small cards available so that you can write down the date and time to give to the parents, with the phone number to use in case they need to reschedule.

It is usual to send two adults on a home visit, both to ensure the health and safety of your employees and so that one person can engage the child in play, to introduce themselves as the person who will be playing with them when they come to nursery or school. The other person can engage the adult in conversation about the child. This shows that you care about each child as an individual and want to treat them as such while they are in your care. It establishes a close working relationship between home and school and is the start of the sharing of information that should continue throughout the child's school career.

There are many examples of pro forma that can be used for collecting information about each pupil during home visits. It is always best if the information can be collected in a non-threatening manner so that the parent feels at their ease. If the parent is relaxed and comfortable in your company, then they are more likely to be open and honest about their child and their needs, rather than defensive.

Some schools adopt the use of first names, particularly in the early years, in order to put families at their ease. Other schools insist on taking a more formal approach and being referred to as 'Miss or Mrs So-and-so' based on concerns that informality will lead to a lack of respect in school. In my experience, the respect shown to you has very little to do with what the children and parents call you. It is more to do with your showing yourself to be trustworthy – respecting their individuality, getting to know them as a family, showing that you care and so forth. You will need to decide how you want the child and their parent to refer to you.

How do you decide what to take with you on home visits?

You will also need to decide whether you will take any resources with you on your home visit. Some schools take a 'goody bag' of resources from school, usually containing a simple jigsaw puzzle, some construction equipment, some pencils, crayons and paper, a cuddly toy. The bag is introduced by 'These are some of our favourite things in nursery [or reception class].' It helps the child make a link between home and school. You can remind them at the end of your visit that they will see and use this equipment when they come to nursery.

Some staff also take a digital camera so that the child can have their photograph taken at home with their parent or carer. This picture is then printed out and displayed on the classroom wall and can also be used as an identifier on the child's coat peg and drawer, again helping them make the link between home and school.

Figures 4.1 and 4.2 show a suggested format for the collection of information from parents to be used during a home visit.

The child can be asked to participate in the home visit by answering a few simple questions about their preferences and the way they like to do things and by completing their first picture for school. Their picture can then be displayed in their classroom before they begin school so that they have it as a reference point of their first day. Staff can talk to the child about the day they visited them at home and remind them of the picture that they drew on that day.

This picture can also be the beginning of a child's learning profile. If you collect regular samples of the child's drawings during their time in the Foundation Stage, you will be able to see their development.

Figure 4.3 represents the booklet filled in by a member of staff in conjunction with the child.

top tip

Beware of the kindness and hospitality of parents – most will offer you some form of refreshment while you are in their home and some will be mortally wounded if you refuse without explaining that you are undertaking up to eight home visits a day and your bladder cannot take the strain!

ABOUT ME	
Name:	Date of birth:
I am usually called:	
Address: Postcode:	
Mother's name: Address: Postcode: Home tel.: Work tel.: Mobile:	Father's name: Address: Postcode: Home tel.: Work tel.: Mobile:
These people will collect me:	
My brothers' and sisters' names and dates of birth are:	
These people are my friends:	
Pre-school group I have been to: Number of full days per week: Number of half days per week:	
At home I speak:	My religion is:
My favourite play activity or interests are:	
My particular comforter is:	
These are my pets:	
Any special medical conditions or allergies:	
My special dietary requirements are:	
This is how I ask for the toilet:	
I am right-handed/left-handed or undecided	
When I am upset I …	

Figure 4.1 About me

During the home visit, in addition to your collecting information from the parent about their child, they also have the opportunity to ask you questions about the school in the comfort of their own environment. The people you send on home visits will therefore need to be well informed about school policy and practice so that they are giving out accurate information.

GENERAL

Is your child happy to play while you are in another room?

Is s/he used to leaving you to visit relatives/friends?

Does s/he do this readily?

Does your child play with other children regularly?

Does s/he have the opportunity to play outside?

Does s/he enjoy listening to stories?

Does s/he enjoy looking at books?

Has s/he a favourite book?

Is s/he used to sharing toys with other children?

Does your child have any particular fears or dislikes?

Is there anything else we should know about your child?

Figure 4.2 General questions for parents/carers

MY FIRST DRAWING FOR SCHOOL

THINGS I LIKE TO DO

My favourite toy is:

My favourite games are:

These are the friends I like to play with:

My favourite TV programme is:

My favourite songs or rhymes are:

Figure 4.3 Booklet filled in by a staff member in conjunction with the child

This is also a good time to reduce the administrative burden usually put on parents on their child's first day at school. You can use the home visit to collect medical and dietary needs, contact information and so on and introduce the parent to the home–school agreement, which might look like this:

As a school we will:

Recognise and develop your child as an individual, independent learner.

Encourage your child to be the best they can be and support their development as a valued member of the school community.

Encourage your child to take care of themselves, their surroundings and others around them.

Provide a balanced, varied and interesting curriculum to meet the individual needs of your child.

Inform you, as parents and carers, of your child's learning and progress at regular meetings and through the end-of-year report.

Be open and welcoming at all times and offer opportunities for you to become involved in the learning life of your child.

Headteacher's signature ....

Child's name ....

As a parent/carer I will:

Ensure that my child attends regularly and comes to school on time and ready to meet the learning challenges before them.

Make sure that I provide a note of explanation if my child is absent.

Ensure that I work with school staff to ensure my child's progress.

Make the school aware of any concerns or problems that might affect my child's work or behaviour.

Support the school's policy and guidelines on behaviour.

Support my child in homework and other opportunities for home learning.

Parent/carer signature/s ....

Date ....

The home–school agreement is usually presented in the form of a pamphlet, which will obviously have the school name and logo on the front. A signed copy should be presented to the parents for their records and another copy should be stored in the child's formal record card at school. The home–school agreement should be completed by parents before their child starts school, even if the child does not enter the school during the Foundation Stage but transfers from another school at a later stage of their school career – it helps to build the bridge between home and school.

CHECKLIST

Here is a checklist for home visits:

● How do you inform parents about your home-visiting policy, so that they don't feel that you are prying?
● How do you arrange your visits with parents and carers?
● Whom do you send on home visits?
● What information will you need to collect so that you have knowledge of each child as an individual learner?
● How do you record the information that you have collected?
● Do you have a pro forma or a schedule of information that you want collected?
● How are you going to engage with the child during the home visit?
● How can you use the home visit to smooth the transition between home and school?

Review your home-visiting policy and practice.
How can you revise your policy and practice to ensure that it supports personalising learning?

Continuing the relationship with parents

This early dialogue between school staff and parents then needs to be continued as their child develops and moves through the school.

Children do not learn only in school and during the hours of 9 a.m. to 3.30 p.m.: learning happens at all times and in all places. You want to ensure that the most is made of every possible learning opportunity but you can't be there for every child all the time. Parents, therefore, play a vital role. You need them to continue to be co-facilitators of learning for their children.

Meeting with parents

This can be facilitated through formal opportunities to meet and discuss the child's progress or through informal opportunities such as day-to-day contact when the children are being brought to or collected from school. It is vital, therefore, that you always ensure that there is a member of staff designated to be free to talk to parents at these times.

Formal opportunities to discuss the child's learning and progress can be centred on the child's development as a learner. Remember, parents hold a vast amount of knowledge about their children as learners outside of the classroom environment, but you will be gathering evidence from your observation of their learning behaviours within the classroom environment. It is very good practice to give feedback on your observations of learning behaviours to the parents/carers of the learners too. They can relate this to the learning behaviours that they see at home and some may well become so fascinated by their children's learning that they will keep a record of observations from play they see at home. This knowledge can then be pooled so that a full picture of the child as a learner in all of their contexts is formed. Sharing observations from home and school is a powerful agenda for a formal parent–teacher meeting to discuss children's learning progress.

This collection of observations should then be used to inform future planning for possible next steps in the child's learning. This becomes an extremely powerful document if it is completed in conjunction with the parents and you can talk about provision for future learning at home and at school.

A gifted advanced-skills teacher for the early years with whom I had the privilege to work devised a pro forma to record these next steps (Figure 4.4). She called them 'possible lines of direction' or PLODs. She called them this because there can be no definite plan made for the child's learning because, as we saw earlier, the child will not always necessarily take a path that has been determined for them by an adult. They will learn in their own way, at their own pace and in their own time.

The PLOD was discussed and completed during a 'formal' parent–staff consultation meeting. These meetings were offered at the beginnings and ends of sessions because parents often found it easier to attend at those times since they were at school anyway dropping off or collecting their children. Staff and parents would discuss and record their observations of the child's learning at home and at school and would then discuss the possible lines of direction and the type of provision that would need to be made in order to move the child on in their learning.

Parents were very positive about taking this shared role with staff and many had their own self-esteem developed as a result of being seen as a partner in the learning of their child, which in turn impacted positively on their child.

Learning environment

You will need to consider the learning environment in terms of the emotional climate you create, the learning space both indoors and outdoors and the use of the time. Personalising learning needs a particular kind of learning environment: children need to feel free to explore and learn in safety, not just physically but emotionally, too. Research shows us that, unless learners have their physical and emotional needs met, they will be unable to learn effectively.

Play at School

Play at Home

Communication, Language and Literacy

Mathematical Development

Possible Lines of Direction for

....
Child's name
....

Creative Development

Personal, Social and Emotional Development

Physical Development

Knowledge and Understanding

Figure 4.4 Possible Lines of Direction planning sheet

The emotional environment

No pupil should ever be made to feel stupid or inadequate. We should be nurturing our pupils to enable them to want to give of their best at all times. There should be no such thing as a school failure or a child who cannot succeed – unless we allow that to happen or even sometimes cause it to happen. Every child should have an entitlement to experience success at school (albeit to varying degrees) and should leave school with a positive self-image and with their self-confidence intact.

A learning environment should be a calm, organised and exciting place to be. As adults we should be aware of the impact we have on the environment. Our mood will impact on each and every pupil and the outcomes of each day. We need to be aware that every word, facial expression or gesture gives messages to those around us. I am not saying that you can never have a bad day or a bad temper, but you need to be aware of the impact that it will have on the learning. It is so easy to be dismissive of a child or their work without ever meaning to, so we need to be conscious of what we say and how we say it. How we speak to each other is vitally important. There should be no place for the casual putdown or sarcasm in our classrooms. Often the children in the Foundation Stage do not understand this low-level wit anyway – it's often used only to make the adult feel better. There should be reciprocal respect in our classrooms and that respect should be earned – adults should not expect or demand it because of their position.

This does not mean that every day has to be a perfect day for every child in the class. You are allowed to be human and have the occasional off day. As long as you remember to apologise afterwards and explain to the child or children why you behaved as you did and said the things you did. If you explain yourself, they will begin to understand the intricacies that make up a human being and it will enable them to understand their own thoughts and actions better and support the development of their social skills, too.

Physical environment

We need to ensure that our learners are comfortable within themselves because they will not be able to learn if they are cold, hungry, thirsty, in need of fresh air or otherwise uncomfortable. These are all-important matters to be considered when constructing a physical environment conducive to learning and they are often sadly overlooked in schools.

To try to meet the physical needs of our learners, we provided fruit and water in all of our classrooms. How this was managed is discussed later in this chapter and also when we discuss Key Stages 1 and 2 in Chapters 5 and 6.

If your school is part of the Healthy Schools Initiative, you may be able to become part of the Fruit for Schools Scheme, which provides free fruit to schools. Contact your Healthy Schools Area Coordinator for further details of this scheme.

Other aspects of the individual's comfort also need to be considered. Some children need to learn in quiet and others need a background noise, so again this needs to be considered within the classroom and areas made available or a compromise reached through discussion with the children, if other learning areas are not available.

Be conscious of the physical environment, whether it is too cold or too hot, whether more fresh air is needed, and make provision for a variety of learning needs in terms of where a child likes to learn and how they like to position themselves for learning, in terms of the furniture you provide.

Maximising space

You need to ensure that space is maximised so that the learners have the room to explore. This will mean considering what furniture you have in your learning environment. You will obviously need storage for your resources and equipment but do you really need a table and chair for every child?

Consider the layout of your learning space – have you made the best use of the space available? You can create more space, sometimes, by pushing most of the storage to the walls of your space, creating a large learning space in the middle. Or you may wish to create several smaller learning spaces for the children by using the furniture to make 'learning bays' where activity-specific resources are stored – but be careful that you are not overly prescriptive in which resources can be used for which activity because that will restrict the decision-making opportunities for the children and may well impede their creativity.

Why not involve the children in organising their learning space? You can ask them at the beginning of each half-term where they would like resources to be kept and in which areas of the room they would like to create learning spaces. Rearranging the learning space and the organisation of resources can often refresh learning if it has become stale.

Don't forget to use your outdoor spaces, too. Many parents are concerned that their children will become ill if they play out in all weathers, so it is up to you to 'educate' the parents that there is no such thing as bad weather, just inappropriate clothing. Part of their preparation for school each day should be to watch or listen to the local weather forecast and provide the right kind of clothing for their child. The outdoor learning space should be accessible to the children at all times of the day (except beginnings and ends of sessions, when the space may be less secure because of parents coming and going), all times of the year and in all weathers.

You may need to build up a stock of 'borrowable' items of clothing and other protection:

- hats for hot days, cold days, wet days;
- jackets, coats and macs;
- wellington boots, sandals and plimsolls; and
- umbrellas.

Jumble sales, charity shops and donations from your families will help you build up your stock of these items.

Maximising time

If children are to be given a high level of choice in what they do, with whom and where, then there are implications for the running of the learning day. The times for group activity will need to be carefully structured over the period of the week to ensure that individualised or personalised opportunities are maximised. This does not mean that all group sessions should be banned but it does mean that group session times should be reviewed to ensure that the best use of learning time is being provided for the children and not just a convenient respite for the adults.

Where you do have group sessions – for example, story time, singing time, news-sharing time – remember to keep it short and focused initially. The time can be gradually extended as the children develop their levels of concentration and their listening skills.

In reception classes where you are beginning to introduce the children to more 'content' – for example, letter sounds and names, number symbols – you can introduce a focused listening time. My staff developed the idea of pulse-learning sessions from Alistair Smith's (1996) suggestion of 'chunking it (learning) down', whereby the adult would give the children an input session for no longer than five minutes. The session would sometimes start with a rap or poem about pulse learning in order to alert the children to the fact that something important was about to happen. You can involve the children in writing their own rhyme or rap. This was one used by our reception-class children and can be sung to the tune of 'Frère Jacques':

> *Are you thinking?*
> *Are you listening?*
> *It's time for PULSE*
> *Time for PULSE*
> *We need to think so we can learn*
> *We need to think so we can learn*
> *It's time for PULSE*
> *Time for PULSE.*

Following the pulse session, the children would be dispersed to work on their own learning activities and would be called back later for a second pulse session of no longer than ten minutes. This can be repeated several times across the day, thereby making content or knowledge more accessible to children.

If you combine the pulse learning sessions with the VAK approach, so that each time you lead a pulse session you use a different learning medium (visual, auditory or kinaesthetic) and draw the children's attention to the fact that they are learning the same information but in a slightly different way, you are supporting them in the development of a very powerful learning strategy. You are also maximising time for children to be engaged in independent learning for themselves rather than spending endless, often fruitless, time listening on the carpet.

Everyday routines within an early-years setting, such as registration and snack time, will need to be thought through, too, if you are to maximise the time available to children to pursue their learning interests. Registration time can be minimised through the use of several techniques.

top tip

Use an egg timer to ensure that your pulse-learning session is only five or ten minutes long.

- One adult can be responsible for marking the children in on seeing them enter the building.
- The children can have a name card that they have to Velcro onto a registration board as soon as they arrive. (This will need to be checked by an adult before completing the register, just in case anyone has put up the wrong name – particularly in the early stages, when the children are just beginning to recognise their name in print.)
- A chart with the child's photos on can be made and laminated so that the children can put a tick by their photo when they arrive.

Snack time is traditionally a time when the children come together and 'waste time' waiting for the drinks and snacks to be given out and then sitting around waiting for everyone else to finish. If we really want to personalise learning for our children, then we should be thinking about their individual needs for food and drink too. Some children will have come to school with little or no breakfast and may well need some nourishment shortly after their arrival; others may have had a huge breakfast and do not need a snack at all. You can personalise the experience by having a drink and snack table that is permanently set up. Jugs of water, milk and bowls of fruit can be put out onto the table and topped up as necessary throughout the session, then the children can access it as and when they need it. They will, of course, need a cup with their name on to reduce the possibility of swapping germs. If a cup is bought for every child on their entry to the school, then they can take them with them to their future classes. They will need to be put through the dishwasher occasionally but otherwise the children can be responsible for doing their own washing up. Some schools choose to provide individual water-drinking bottles rather than cups, to avoid spillage. Managing snack time in this way eliminates the need for this group time and maximises learning time and also meets the individual needs of children regarding their nourishment needs.

Outdoor environment

Children in the Foundation Stage should have ready access to their outdoor learning environment in all weathers and at all times of the year. The outdoors should not just be for boisterous play and the use of outdoor toys, though obviously that is an important part of learning to manage themselves physically. The outdoor environment should reflect the indoor learning environment and the children should have access to the same range of activities outdoors as in, so if they want to paint outdoors or sit quietly and look at a book the environment should enable this.

CHECKLIST

- Is the learning environment you have created an emotionally safe place for the children to be?
- How does the learning environment enable your children to continue to develop as independent learners?
- Have you maximised learning opportunities by using the space and time available to you creatively?
- Can the children use the outdoor environment for all aspects of their learning, or is it just for boisterous and messy play?
- Is the outdoor environment easily accessible to the children?
- Is the learning environment too hot/too cold/too stuffy/too dark?
- Do the children have easy access to drinks of water?
- How do you ensure that children have access to healthy snacks?
- Is there adequate space for the children to play and learn?

Review your classroom environment.
What can you do to ensure that it facilitates personalising learning?

Classroom provision and use of resources

Classrooms come in a variety of shapes and sizes and in a variety of locations; but, if you are considering embarking on personalising learning, then note that there are certain elements of classroom provision and the use of resources that you will need to consider:

- adult–pupil ratio;
- the types of resources to provide;
- the storage of resources; and
- the use of display.

Adults are a significant influence on the learning of children and the more adults that you are able to have in a classroom supporting and facilitating learning, the more effective the learning should be.

The kind of resources you provide and how they are stored will impact on the types of activity in which the children can become engaged. If you buy toys and resources that have limited use, children will be limited in their play and learning. If you provide resources that can be used in a variety of ways and for a variety of purposes, you are creating opportunities for the children to be creative and make choices.

Resources need to be stored so that the children can readily access them, so that they are developing their independence.

Display not only makes the learning environment look more attractive and appealing, but can also support learning and help young children make the link between home and school. You can also use display to enhance the positive self-image of the children by valuing their work and displaying it for others to see.

Adult–pupil ratio

In most early-years settings it is usual to have two adults to thirty pupils. If you want to develop personalising learning, you will need to consider whether you have the resources to increase the number of adults that you have available so that you can staff all of your learning spaces and have at least one person designated as the 'observer of learning'. I would suggest that you need at least three adults: one to work indoors, one to work outdoors and one to observe. This system runs on a rota so that everyone has an opportunity to work in all areas across the working week.

You can, of course, always use additional adults such as students and volunteers or parent helpers to boost your ratios even further. But, before any of these additional adults are 'let loose' in your learning space, they should have some understanding of the way in which you are working. It takes only one careless word or intervention to undo all of your good work in developing your children as independent learners.

This can be done informally, by chatting to the early-years staff or by formal observation followed by discussion of the way in which you work, or by an even more formalised training course that you could offer. It is up to you to decide the best way forward to ensure that all the adults working alongside your developing learners are going to be supporting the way you work and not undermining it.

top tip

To assist additional adults working with you, you can put up learning posters next to learning areas that will support them in what they are looking for in terms of extending the learning within that area. They should always be asked for feedback at the end of the session so that their observations can be fed into your records.

BLOCK PLAY		
Physical development	**Intellectual development**	**Social/Emotional development**
• Can lift and carry large bricks • Can place bricks in tall structures • Can place bricks to make linear structures • Makes enclosed structures • Can balance blocks • Combines different sizes and shapes effectively • Makes complex constructions • Can place small bricks accurately	• Can talk about their constructions and how they made them • Can explain about what has been built • Can think of solutions to problems that arise • Can sort the blocks by shape and size • Can use appropriate language to describe their construction	• Can share materials and space • Shows interest in the ideas of others • Seeks adult support or reassurance • Concentrates well on task • Can play cooperatively with others • Willingly helps to tidy up

ART-AND-CRAFT MATERIALS		
Physical development	**Intellectual development**	**Social/Emotional development**
• Has good hand–eye coordination • Can control materials • Can manipulate tools with accuracy	• Beginning to solve problems • Can find materials required and tidy them up • Can estimate size and shape • Can measure, match, sort, count • Listens well and interprets instructions • Observes and copies • Can adapt ideas	• Can share materials and ideas • Can communicate ideas and feelings • Can share work space and tools • Developing aesthetic awareness • Can appreciate other people's ideas and work • Shows satisfaction at completing a task

SAND AND WATER PLAY		
Physical development	**Intellectual development**	**Social/Emotional development**
• Can manipulate tools with dexterity • Has good hand–eye coordination • Can tip and pour accurately • Developing muscular strength to lift and carry	• Can sort out materials • Can remember what has been done • Can add new ideas • Experiments with materials • Discovers important properties of materials • Describes what they have done • Makes deliberate choices over materials	• Watches other children at work • Works alongside other children • Shares work space and materials with others • Negotiates over use of equipment • Concentrates on activity • Replaces materials and tools after use • Involves others in their discoveries

Figure 4.5 Learning posters

Learning posters

Learning posters can be made to be placed in each working area of the nursery or reception classroom. The posters can contain information about the type of learning behaviours that may be displayed in that area. They can assist the adults in recording their observations. Figure 4.5 shows a few examples of posters.

Materials and resources

If your classroom is set up in a way that prevents the children from being able to access materials and resources as and when they need them, they cannot become independent. So, here are a few ideas about resource storage.

- Resources must be stored in low, accessible places.
- Resources must be labelled with word and picture (you can cut these out of catalogues) so that the children can see what is in the drawer or box.
- Boxes and drawers must not be overloaded so that they are too heavy for children to lift and carry for themselves.
- It helps the child to become independent at tidy-away time if there are silhouettes stuck onto places to which resources should be returned – tidying up then becomes a matching exercise.

There should be a range of resources made available to the children so that they can have whatever they need to fulfil their self-determined learning tasks. The learning resources should not only be the shiny, plastic, expensive toys and equipment that you find in early-years shops and catalogues, but there should be a range of natural materials and everyday objects for the children to use imaginatively and creatively too. These should include:

- cards, envelopes, range of writing papers, forms, magazines, notepads, catalogues, etc.;
- conkers;
- corks;
- curtain rings;
- hair rollers;
- junk materials – small bags and boxes;
- leaves;
- old keys;
- ribbons, buttons, wool, material offcuts;
- shells;
- tins and containers of all sizes;
- wooden laundry pegs;
- wrapping paper;
- wood, nails, screws, nuts and bolts, etc.

Children can be involved in collecting these materials for their school or nursery. Whenever they go to the bank or post office, they could bring back some forms. They can bring in magazines and catalogues from home. They can bring in junk materials from home and add them to the school collection.

It is also a good idea to have larger items for children to use in their play too. For example,

- bread trays;
- milk crates;
- plastic pipes;
- logs;
- old sheets, tarpaulins, blankets, etc.;
- planks.

You can ask your DIY enthusiasts or local tradespeople to bring in pipes, planks and the like, left over from their projects. If you make links with your local supermarket or dairy, they will let you have bread trays and milk crates.

top tip

Music can be used to great effect to help you 'frame' tidying-up time. It also saves the adults' voices, because they don't need to give the instruction to start tidying up: they just press 'play' on their CD or tape player. We found that our foundation-stage children responded really well to 'A Spoonful of Sugar' from *Mary Poppins*. The music signifies that it is time to tidy up and you have the length of the piece of music to complete the task. The adults can then be part of the tidying-up team, modelling good tidying-up behaviour for the children.

With these larger materials the children can make their own climbing frames, dens and so forth, rather than rely on pre-made climbing frames that restrict their imagination. They can also make something different to play with every time instead of having the same old toy every day.

Display

You will obviously want to brighten your classroom with the use of display. Make sure that you display children's work and not adult work. It is always a temptation to draw templates for children to colour or stick things onto, but that is not providing them with opportunities to personalise their learning. As we saw earlier, the resources should be made available to the children and it should be their decision as to what they produce. Seeing that you value their work enough to spend time mounting and displaying it for others to see is a powerful motivator for most children. Getting the children to bring things in from home for your displays also helps to make a valuable link for the children between learning at home and school – photographs, artefacts, etc.

Displays should be (ideally):

- at an appropriate height for the children, so that they can see and talk about their work;
- interactive so that the children can touch artefacts (you will need to have understandings about not spoiling other people's work by touching it);
- changed often to stimulate interest; and
- displayed attractively to show that you value the children's work.

CHECKLIST

- How many adults will you need in a classroom that will support personalising learning?
- Are children enabled to make active decisions about where and how they learn?
- Is the classroom a safe place to be – not just in terms of health and safety but in terms of emotional safety?
- Is the space for learning maximised? Is there readily available access to the outdoor environment?
- Is the time for learning maximised?
- Are the daily routines supporting personalising learning by enabling the learners to be independent?
- Are resources easily accessible? Is there a range of resources available?
- Are the displays interactive and at the right height for the children?

Review your classroom provision.

What changes do you need to introduce so that your classroom provision facilitates personalising learning?

Curriculum

A curriculum for personalising learning would have the child at the centre and develop in response to the child's learning needs. 'The Foundation Stage Areas of Learning and Early Learning Goals' support personalising learning very well. They consider the development of the whole child, starting with the personal, social and emotional development. They provide a broad framework in which foundation-stage staff can develop a variety of activities and learning opportunities in response to the children's developing needs.

For personalising learning, the curriculum needs to be flexible in order to meet individual learning needs.

You can use the 'Foundation Stage Areas of Learning and Early Learning Goals' and consider the Stepping Stones that provide development guidelines and plan your curriculum in those areas. Following your observations of learning in your classroom, so that you understand the needs of every individual, you can highlight different aspects of each area of learning in your planning and provide a range of resources that will enable the children to develop skills, knowledge and understanding in those areas.

Before the introduction of the 'Foundation Stage Areas of Learning and Early Learning Goals', my staff and I devised our own early-years core curriculum. Table 4.1 shows what it looked like.

Learning activities

When considering the range of learning activities that are made available to the children, you will need to ensure that any activities chosen reflect your philosophy about developing children as individual independent learners.

If you are going to personalise learning for the children, then each child will need the freedom to respond to their learning environment and develop at their own pace and in their own way. Their learning development will all be at different stages, dependent on their early-learning experiences, their emotional state, their motivation and so on. It would not be possible, nor should it be expected, that the adults should provide an individualised programme of learning activities for each child – that is not what personalising learning is all about. Providing learning experiences for anyone is a very hit-or-miss affair, anyway, because each learner will bring their own personal approach and prior learning to any experience and may have completely different approaches to an activity from the one you had planned.

To ensure that you are really personalising learning for your pupils, most of the learning activities available to the children should be chosen and directed by the children themselves. This does not mean that you never introduce new activities or have adult-led activities – these still have their place. But the majority of the time should be made available for the children to learn by exploring their environment and the resources within it.

The more 'real' the learning opportunity, the more likely the children are to engage in the learning activities. They need to be able to see the purpose of engaging in learning and then they will be more motivated to engage in developing their learning skills. The skill of the adult learning facilitator is in providing a range of opportunities that present the children with real reasons for engaging.

SKILL/ATTITUDE	KNOWLEDGE AND UNDERSTANDING
Self-management Independence and responsibility Recognising and managing potential risks to safety	• Getting dressed, undressed independently • Personal hygiene and personal safety • Distinguishing between, and discussing, feelings • Handling tools, objects, construction and malleable materials safely • Developing awareness of basic safety rules in the home and school • Ability to select and use activities and resources independently • Taking responsibility for own actions • Beginning to develop an understanding of the difference between 'right' and 'wrong' • Developing a sense of routine
Respect for people, environment and property	• Opportunity to experience different cultures/festivals • Developing an awareness of individual differences • Respecting and being responsible for their immediate environment, both indoors and outdoors • Developing an awareness of their immediate locality • Valuing each other's language
Healthy lifestyle	• Developing an awareness of healthy eating and the benefits of exercise in order to remain healthy
Playing an active role in society	• Caring for one another • Valuing and taking an active role in school life • Developing an understanding of the importance of turn taking
Managing relationships in a variety of contexts	• Becoming aware of the impact of your actions on others' feelings • Developing the ability to play harmoniously • Ability to discuss the Golden Rules
Effective communication	• Developing the ability to speak and listen in small and large groups • Understanding the need to speak with clarity and audibility
Problem-solving ability	• Beginning to develop confidence and familiarity with the computer • Developing basic mouse skills • Being confident to try new activities • Being confident to solve own problems
Research skills	• Beginning to understand the difference between fiction and non-fiction • Willing to try to find out for themselves
Thinking skills	• Developing the ability to complete activities • Sorting • Sequencing • Comparing • Contrasting • Being encouraged to give simple reasoning • Being encouraged to ask questions • Being encouraged to develop imaginative skills through play • Being encouraged to develop simple evaluation skills
Self-evaluation	• Being encouraged to reflect on their learning • Being encouraged to reflect on what they do well

Table 4.1 An early-years curriculum

New activities or adult-led activities can be used if you want to introduce a new skill, technique or resource to the children, but should be resisted at all other times, other than formalised group learning, e.g. singing, story time, PE or other group physical activity.

The role of the adults is to provide stimulating resources and enough time and space for learning, and to observe the learning as it happens so that they can modify future provision to meet the developing needs of the learners. You should also get involved in playing alongside the children but try to resist the temptation to lead the play in the direction you want it to go – you should let yourself be led by their play. You can support their language development by talking as you play about what you are doing, and you can ask them questions about their play and learning, but try to do this in as unobtrusive a manner as you can. Remember, in order to personalise learning you need the learning to come from the child. The children need to decide for themselves.

Developing children as decision makers

In setting up your classroom for personalising learning, you are looking at ways of building upon the independence and decision-making opportunities in which they have been engaging during their early childhood at home or in childcare. In order for the child to make their own decisions and continue to develop their independence, there must be decisions to be made in their new setting. It is important that you build on the skills that they bring with them, rather than work on regimenting them and making them 'toe the line'.

If children are to develop as independent lifelong learners, then one of the most important skills to learn is that of decision making and making choices. As they grow older, they need to make choices of subjects to choose in secondary school and career choices as well as life choices. In order to become proficient at decision making and making choices, they need to develop the skill early and practise it in a safe environment.

Building in choice

If you are going to adopt personalising learning, you need to build real choice into your daily provision and then also work with the children to develop the skill of choosing, otherwise how will they know what to do?

What do I mean by choice? I am talking about children from a very young age being expected to make decisions for themselves about how they operate within their learning environment. We often underestimate the ability of children to reason and make appropriate choices, but, if given the opportunity, they become highly skilled at doing just that. It can start quite simply, for example, one very wet and rainy morning in the nursery garden, a boy stood at the top of the slide. The slide was obviously wet and the child was obviously considering his options. An adult, playing with a group of children at the other side of the garden, noticed him standing there and made eye contact with him. 'What are you going to do?' was all that she said to him, not 'Get down from there before you get wet.' He stood for a while longer pondering the possibilities and eventually turned around and came down the steps. The important thing here is not that he didn't get wet trousers but that he made his own decision about what to do, and, had he chosen to come down the slide anyway, then he would have had to deal with the consequences of his decision.

This choice making was not accidental. The adults working in the nursery need to encourage the children to develop the skill. They spend a lot of time talking through the issues and consequences of making choices and have the confidence to leave the child to make the final decision.

If children are to feel secure about making their own decisions, they need to be in an emotional environment that supports and encourages them. We must be wary as adults that our own needs do not replace the needs of the child. We need to use language carefully, to encourage children to participate fully in making choices for themselves and take their responses seriously. We must be careful never to ridicule or put down a child with a glance or a word or by ignoring them. The learning environment (which is everywhere) should be supportive of the learners; it should be a 'no-putdown zone'. We must respond in a positive way, engaging them in discussion, following the child's lead through the conversation, never imposing our own agenda on them. We must encourage the children really to think things through so that they can see an issue through from possible action to its consequences.

During conversation with young children, it is best to ask open-ended questions so that the child has the freedom to respond in a way that is right for them. You should aim to use open questions that engage the child in giving a full answer rather than closed questions that can be answered with a 'yes' or 'no' – questions such as:

- 'What have you been doing?'
- 'Can you tell me about…?'
- 'What will you do next?'

We need to create opportunities for the children to make real decisions. Questions such as 'What are you going to learn at nursery today?' will provide children with the opportunity to make those decisions for themselves. This can be done on an individual basis initially, but then – since you will want to help the children develop their sense of belonging and class identity – you will introduce some group times when they can share the outcomes of their decision making.

This can be done at the beginnings and ends of sessions as a circle-time or group-time activity. The children are brought together and are introduced to the concepts of taking turns and listening carefully to others. Because the children are sitting in a circle they can see each other more clearly, facilitating effective communication. You can introduce turn taking by having an artefact, such as a ball, a soft toy or – my staff's favourite – a painted wooden egg. The 'rule' is introduced that you can speak only when you are holding the artefact.

Puppets can be used to great effect during circle time, particularly for those children who find it difficult to talk in large groups. If a puppet is used by the adult leading the session and the puppet asks the children the question 'What are you going to learn in nursery today?', the children can take it in turns to give a reply. You would obviously not expect a response from every child in one sitting: this would take far too long and the children would become restless. But you would need to ensure that across the week that every child has had the opportunity of contributing to the discussion if they choose to do so. (Some may choose not to take part in these discussions and this can be for a variety of reasons. It is something that you would want to note and discuss with their parent or carer.)

You can then introduce the children to asking further questions about their planned learning, through the same technique of using the puppet. The puppet can ask:

- 'Who are you going to work with to day?'
- 'Are you going to work inside or outside?'
- 'What materials will you need?'
- 'Will you need some help or do you want to work on your own?'

You can then ask the other children if they have any questions. Initially, they will use the ones that the puppet has introduced them to, but eventually they will come up with questions of their own.

This group activity can be used at the ends of sessions, too, so that children begin to develop the language of review and learn about evaluating their work and play. The puppet would ask such questions as:

- 'What did you like best about what you did?'
- 'What did you find hard or difficult?'
- 'Who did you like to work with?'
- 'Who helped you or did you work by yourself?'
- 'Would you do anything differently if you were going to do it again?'
- 'How did you feel while you were working?'

This process introduces very young children to the concept of 'plan – do – review' and begins to give them the vocabulary they will need to describe their learning. If you use the process consistently across the Foundation Stage, the children should develop some quite sophisticated understandings of how they like to learn, with whom and where. It is not to say that these very early choices will remain with them as they grow and mature throughout their school career, but these early observations are often reflected in their later learning behaviours.

The information collected by the adults during this process can be reflected in the provision of resources and activities too, as well as providing essential assessment information that should be recorded in a child's individual learning record. We'll look at more about what records to keep later.

What to do when things go wrong

If we want children to be decision makers we must be prepared for some mishaps. Sometimes they will make the wrong decision and it is then the adult's role to talk through what has happened and ask the child what they might have done differently. It is important that in the conversation the child should not end up feeling 'blamed' for what went wrong. You are merely exploring the situation with them and getting them to think about what happened and why. In this way, they will start to make the connection between their actions and the consequences.

You will also need to keep a handy supply of spare clothes, newspapers for mopping up spills, clean towels for showering and a large supply of patience. Remember that you are trying to develop a 'no-blame culture' so that the children are prepared to take learning risks. If the risk backfires, the child needs to be talked, calmly, through what has happened and what might be done in the future to ensure that the 'mistake' doesn't happen again. In this way, you are helping them grow and learn from their mistakes, which is a lifelong learning skill.

Developing the five Rs

1 Resilience

Building in opportunities for children to develop persistence or 'stickability': You can do this by being there while they are learning and encouraging them with your feedback on how well they are doing. You can expand their concentration and application by asking them what they might do next while they are engaged in a learning activity. Or you can extend their persistence through your provision of adult-led activities, which can expand in terms of their complexity so that the children need to spend longer working at them or need to draw more deeply on their skills and develop new skills in order to complete a task.

Instead of providing a pristine sandpit with endless plastic toys and tools, why not just provide an area of ground for the children to dig and explore. They will soon go hunting for implements to help them with their digging, discovering for themselves what works best; and, if you spend time 'burying' various bits of treasure for them to discover, you will keep reinvigorating their curiosity. When they have found their treasure, ask them to tell you about it. Who left it there? What do they think it was used for? You have created a wonderful learning opportunity, which will go wherever the children decide it will go. You will find that they will spend 'hours' at an activity like this, becoming self-motivated and developing their 'stickability'.

Building in opportunities for children to be adventurers: This is also about creating open-ended learning opportunities – differentiation by outcome. For example, everyone might be asked to do a painting of a daffodil. You don't tell the children what to do and how to do it because you will end up with thirty almost identical paintings. Why not just provide the paint and paper and stand back to see what happens?

Building in opportunities for children to deal with difficulties: This is about standing back and letting children problem-solve for themselves. The adult role in this process is to ask the question, 'What are you going to do about…?' This enables the child rather than making them reliant on someone else to solve their problems for them. They will develop a positive attitude to dealing with difficulties and extend their range of possible strategies for managing and coping.

Building in opportunities for children to deal with confusion: In the way that adults should not solve problems for children, nor should they sanitise the world so that the confusion is removed and children never have to deal with it. It is only by experiencing confusion and working through it for yourself that you can make sense of the world and your place in it.

Adults should be available to support children in their deliberations and may need to ask questions to enable the children to organise their thoughts, but don't fall into the trap of being expected to provide all the answers. You should model your response to confusion, willingly declaring that sometimes you don't know why things have happened like that and also sometimes model your inability to decide what to do about things. Externalise your thought processes by talking aloud while you work though uncertainty and confusion. This will help the child learn some of the processes involved.

2 Resourcefulness

Make sure that your learning environment is exciting and well resourced by ensuring that there is a wide range of learning tools available to the children and providing a wide range of open-ended learning activities; or, better still, encourage the children to make decisions about what they would like to do.

If you are setting out an adult-led activity to introduce new skills or equipment to the children, make sure that you don't have all the necessary tools available on the table, so that the children have to go looking for the right tool for the job in hand. In this way, you are assisting them in developing their creativity and independence – two vital skills in resourcefulness.

3 Reflectiveness

Use group sessions or carpet times at the start of learning sessions to encourage the children to think about what they are going to do and at the end of learning sessions to think about what they have done.

Another effective way of developing reflectiveness in children in a reception class is to use 'chat partners' during carpet time. When you are asking a question or requiring a response or ideas from the children, give them a few minutes to chat to the person next to them, to come with some answers or ideas together first. Then ask for hands up or select a few representative pairs to share their thinking. Others can be asked whether they agree or disagree by showing a thumbs-up or thumbs-down hand signal.

By using chat partners in this way, you are building in thinking time – the children clarify their thoughts during the chat time with their partners and have a clear idea about what they want to say before they are asked to make a contribution in the large group.

4 Remembering

Use a range of techniques with the children so that they discover the best way for them of remembering things.

Practice, repetition and review work. For example, if you want the children to learn letter names and sounds, build in lots of short bursts over the day when children are asked to remember.

5 Responsiveness

This is about helping the children to manage change and uncertainty with confidence. Encourage them to 'have a go' at things and be confident that the outcome will be fine. When things go wrong, ensure that you remember that you have adopted a no-blame culture so that children are not frightened to make mistakes, but get them involved in clearing up the chaos caused so that they know what needs to be done in each circumstance.

Adults need to model excitement about the possibilities of getting involved in doing something new and talk about their responses to things that don't go right.

Reading, writing, numbers and ICT

While advocating personalising learning, there are some key skills that need to be learned, otherwise children's future learning careers will be severely prejudiced. Children must still learn such skills as how to read, how to write, how to manipulate numbers, how to use ICT effectively.

In the Foundation Stage most of these key skills can be 'taught' through play and the use of first-hand experience.

Reading

Children need to be surrounded by the written word (in the main community languages for your area). They need to see the adults around them using print to help them in their daily lives, e.g. reading newspapers and magazines, reading ingredients from a recipe book, reading items of food packaging while shopping.

You will need to provide a wide range of books (this should contain fiction and non-fiction books on a range of subjects) and other reading material (magazines, catalogues, timetables, for instance) so that the children have a wide choice of how they interact with print. Your book area should provide children with a range of seating options, too. Some children like to sit upright on a chair to read; others like to lie on their backs on large floor cushions; other children like to lie on the floor on their stomachs. They will engage more readily with the reading material if they can do it in a way that is comfortable for them.

The children should be read to daily – some children will like to share books with you on an individual basis, others will be happy to share in small or large groups. Some children will bring in books from home to share with you; others may need you to provide books for them to take home to share with their family. Some will be starting to connect print on the page with the spoken word; others will not be at that stage. In order to personalise the experience of learning to be a reader, you will need to know how each individual interacts with print. You will find out by watching the children interact with books and by engaging in conversation as you share books with the children.

In the reception class, most children will be ready to be introduced to individual letter names and sounds. You can do this by using a PULSE session and by introducing one letter sound and name at a time. My staff particularly liked 'Jolly Phonics' (see www.jollylearning.co.uk), because each letter sound (for auditory learners) was accompanied by an action to help children learn the correct letter formation (for kinaesthetic learners) and a character (for visual learners). Each letter also had its own rhyme or jingle that the children could learn too.

One way to help parents support the learning of phonics is to provide each child with a sound book. The 'Jolly Phonics' letter for the week can be stuck in the book – they are from a photocopiable resource book, and it gives the parents the action and the character rhyme – and the children can be told to go home and teach the letter sound and formation to their parents. Explaining something to someone else helps fix the learning in your brain.

Writing

A system of developmental writing fits in best with personalising learning. You will need to have a well-resourced writing area that contains:

- a range of papers (size, colours, shapes, textures);
- a range of writing implements (pens, pencils, crayons, chalks, etc.);
- alphabet frieze;
- key-word vocabulary poster; and
- children's name cards.

You should also provide a range of opportunities for children to get engaged in writing. The simplest way is to ask them always to ensure that they put their name on their art and other work. They can also be encouraged to make a list of things that they will need before starting, say, to construct a model. (You will, of course, have been role-modelling this for them by making lists during your working day.) Your home corner can have a notepad by the phone so that the children can take messages as part of their play. You can have lists by popular activities such as the computer or listening station so that the children have to write their names on the list in order to secure a turn. If they are playing competitive games, they can keep a list of top scorers or other statistics. There are limitless opportunities that can be created for the children to engage in writing activities in a meaningful context.

Obviously, most children, at this stage, will not be writing the correct letters in the right order to form recognisable words – indeed some may still be at the 'scribbling' stage – but nevertheless they should be encouraged to 'read' their writing at every opportunity.

In the early stages of a child's development as a writer, you will probably find that they choose to write using capital letters initially. This is because straight lines are much easier to form than curves. You should accept a child's writing, however it is formed at this stage, but ensure that you are modelling the formation of lowercase letters in your writing.

As children become more interested in writing 'properly' they can be shown the correct letter formation ('Jolly Phonics' helps with this too). Writing practice doesn't always have to be with pencil on paper. The children can practice their letter formation with:

- chalk on the playground floor (they love the challenge of having to make the letters as big as they can so that they can run or walk around them);
- paintbrushes and water on the playground floor;
- fingers in paint on tabletops;
- fingers in wet sand or mud;
- fingers in cornflour and water paste; and
- with paint on paper.

By the time they choose to do it with pencil on paper, the letter formations will be well and truly fixed in their brains.

Number

Children can be introduced to numbers through the use of song and rhyme and through their everyday play activities. Again, adults will be role-modelling how they use numbers in their daily routines and using every opportunity to count and sequence numbers so that children see them doing it in real situations. The children can then be encouraged to join in with the counting.

You can also introduce games that will involve counting. For example, use bean bags or soft balls for target practice. You provide a range of differently shaped and sized containers and the children have to throw their balls or bean-bags into them and count up how many they scored. You can extend this as the child becomes proficient at managing small numbers by drawing a target with numbered scoring areas, and the child would have three balls or bean bags to throw at the target and they would be expected to count up their score.

Board games are very useful at encouraging children to count, too, as they move their counters around the board and read the number from the dice (start with dotted dice so that children have to count, and then, as you introduce the number symbols to the children, you can use a die with printed numbers).

ICT

Children will need to be shown how to use the class computer. They can be introduced to simple games that will help them become familiar with the keyboard and mouse. By the end of the Foundation Stage, they should be confident to draw and print pictures using art packages and they should be able to save their work in their own work folder.

Observation of learning

Early-years practice has built up an excellent grounding and years of experience in observation of children's learning. There are many excellent frameworks for recording your observations and starting to understand what you are seeing.

It is only by observing learning taking place that you will begin to develop knowledge of each of the children as an individual learner. During the Foundation Stage, the children won't have developed the language or maturity of understanding to enable them to describe their own learning needs, so it is vital that you observe their learning and provide them with some feedback on what you see. In this way, you will be supporting their development as learners and helping them develop the language to describe themselves and their needs.

The context of your observations

When you are observing, in order to develop your understanding of each individual as a learner, you will want to consider the following:

- Was the learning self-initiated or led by another (adult or child)?
- What was the stimulus for the learning? Did it come from the child, a provided resource, a situation, a comment?
- Where is the child learning? Do they have a preferred setting for their learning to take place?
- What are they actually doing? Record in detail, particularly trying to capture anything of significance that shows learning taking place in what the child either does or says.
- How did the child react?
- What learning behaviours did they show?
- With whom does the child share their learning?
- What does the child do at the end of their learning activity?
- How do they manage transitions from one activity to another?

You will not be observing or recording on all of these aspects during each observation, but, if your adults are alert to spot key learning moments in a child's day and record them, you will soon build up an accurate profile of the child as a learner at that point in time. You can then modify your picture of the child as their learning behaviours develop as they mature.

Most early-years settings will have their own preferred system for organising their observations of their pupils' learning behaviours. Here are just a few examples:

- have 'focus children' for that day or week;
- have one of the adults assigned specifically to stand back and observe children at work, recording anything of interest that they see on a variety of pro formas;
- have focus activities or resource areas and record what happens there (particularly useful if you have just introduced a new resource); and
- have the areas of learning on the wall and use sticky notes with scribbled notes on them, which are then later transferred to the learning profile for each child.

You will also need to decide how your observations are recorded. You can use sticky notes, blank sheets of paper, a journal or diary divided into days of the week, a pad by each play or resource area or have specifically designed pro formas.

However you decide to record your observations, always remember to record:

- the name of the child or children whom you are observing;
- the date and time of your observation;
- the period of time your observation covers;
- the context of the observation; and
- who made the observation.

A suggested pro forma for observations is given as Figure 4.6.

Date: Observation made by:	Start time: Stop time:
Focus child/children:	
Context: setting and stimulus	
Observation: what the child does and what the child says	
Key outcomes:	
Possible next steps:	

Figure 4.6 Suggested pro forma for observations

Whichever way you choose to record your observations, it is vital that the adults share their developing knowledge of each child as a learner. This can be done in short but focused end-of-session or end-of-day meetings where significant breakthroughs in learning have taken place. To ensure that you are not always discussing the same children who command a lot of attention, you should ensure that you have discussed every child at least once a fortnight.

Don't forget that writing is not the only way of recording observations: you can use photographs (a digital camera is a must for every classroom), drawings or diagrams and video and audiotape recordings.

It is always best to record your observations as they are happening. In that way you will get a rich picture of the child's learning – if you leave it and think that you will remember to record it later, you will lose some of that richness.

What do I do with the data from my observations?

Initially, it may feel as if you are collecting lots of observations of the child working for the sake of it. But, if you collect your observations consistently over time, you will start to see patterns of behaviour emerge; you will see details of their character emerge; you will begin to get a real insight into them as individual learners. You should start to see:

- whether they prefer to work alone, alongside or interacting with others;
- whether they prefer to work predominantly indoors or outdoors;
- whether they prefer construction activities, social activities, physical activities or whatever;
- whether they use language to describe their play or prefer to play in silence;
- whether they spend extended periods of time on certain activities or flit from one to another in rapid succession, never really engaging with anything; and
- whether they are reliant on adults for guidance or are self-determining in their play

This knowledge helps you build up your picture of each child as an individual learner. It should then be recorded in a learning profile for each child. The learning profile can be as simple as a blank sheet of paper headed with the child's name and date of birth, on which you record and date significant developments in their learning. A more detailed format can be a sheet divided into the six areas of learning from the early-learning goals and you can record your observations of learning under those headings or you can have a more complex format that covers aspects of the child's development as a learner. Figure 4.7 gives an example of such a format.

It is for you to decide which way you want to keep your learning profiles. But it is important to remember that they should be updated often – I would be concerned if you had not been able to record something for each child in a two-week period.

Feedback on your observations to children and parents

Observations are of no use to support your working towards personalising learning unless they are shared with the children and parents. It is vital to share your understanding of individual learners with the individuals concerned so that they can modify their emerging picture of themselves through your feedback.

Name: Male/female DOB: Started nursery on: Left-/right-handed	

Health • information from registration form (e.g. hearing and sight) • updates on any intervention from health agencies	**Coordination** • gross motor skills • fine motor skills
Emotional development • copes with feelings • expresses feelings verbally • expresses feelings physically	**Response to learning experiences** • prefers to self-direct or be directed • independent use of resources • investigates their environment freely • confident to try new experiences • experiments freely and with confidence
Confidence and independence • coping with change • self-help skills • dependence on adults/peers	**Concentration and motivation** • ability to stay on task • ability to listen • self-motivating
Communication • clarity of speech • ability to engage in dialogue with adults/peers • quality of language – single words, monosyllabic or sentences, questioning	**Relationships** • interacts with other children • plays (solitary, alongside, cooperatively) • interacts with adults

Comments: • parent/carer or key worker comments as appropriate to include special talents

Key worker:	Parent/carer:	Date:

Figure 4.7 An example of a learning profile

This can be done during a group session or individually following learning activities, particularly if you have been working alongside a group or an individual.

To give individual feedback you will need to be specific in your use of language. It is no good saying to the child, 'You worked well today.' They will learn nothing about themselves from such a comment. You need to be specific in what they did that was good working: 'You really listened well today – I could tell because you knew exactly what to do'; or 'You worked hard at your work with the building bricks today – I could tell because you kept building for a long time and you didn't give in even when your building fell down.' The more specific you can be with your feedback, the more they will learn about themselves as learners. I would always finish a feedback session by asking the child for their comments too – they might have a completely different view of how they were working and you won't know unless you ask them what they think.

To give feedback during a group session, you will still need to be specific in what good learning behaviours the child exhibited, but by doing it during a group session you are providing opportunities for others to hear about it, too. You can finish the session by reminding the children that if they want to be good at … (building blocks, for example) they might ask for some help from such-and-such a child, because they are very good at it. This will share some of the expertise that the children are developing and it will also reinforce a positive self-image for the child who is the expert.

It is very good practice to give feedback on learning behaviours to the parents/carers of the learners, too. They can relate this to the learning behaviours that they see at home and some may well become so fascinated by their children's learning that they will keep a record of observations from play they see at home. This knowledge can then be pooled so that a full picture of the child as a learner in all of their contexts is formed.

This collection of observations should then be used to inform future planning for possible next steps in the child's learning. This becomes an extremely powerful document if it is shared with the parents and you can talk about provision at home and at school.

Record keeping

You will need to keep records on the children's development as learners. For personalising learning, it is important that you have a detailed knowledge of each individual and their learning preferences, their learning 'styles', their strengths and areas that need further development so that you can make the right kind of provision in order to ensure further learning progress. Remember that you are developing the learning to fit the child, not providing 'blind'.

By keeping full and up-to-date records of each child's individual learning profile, you are:

● ensuring that you are recognising each individual's changing learning needs; and
● providing evidence of each child's learning development.

Checklists and tick sheets are not going to give you a detailed picture of each child's development as an individual learner. You need to keep detailed records for each child. There are several ways of doing this. You can:

● keep a running profile on a piece of paper for each child that is added to on a regular basis;
● keep a running profile for each child that is organised into the foundation-stage areas of learning;
● keep a portfolio for each child in the form of a scrapbook that has samples of their work in it (remember, this can be photos, video- and audiotape, too); or
● keep a portfolio for each child in the form of a loose-leaf file.

In whatever format you decide to keep your records, you must ensure that your knowledge of the development of your learners is recorded in the same format for each child. You will, of course, have more records for some children than for others, particularly if they have special learning needs or are causing you some concern, but you should ensure that all aspects of learning are covered for all children.

Planning for learning

Although you are working towards personalising learning for your pupils, it is still the responsibility of the adults to plan for learning. Remember that personalising learning is not about abdicating all responsibility for learning and leaving the children to get on with it for themselves. Indeed, if you are going to personalise learning successfully, you will need to work harder at planning in order to be more responsive to the children's learning needs.

There are many and varied formats used in the Foundation Stage to record the planning of learning activities. The best of them are reviewed and amended daily in order to meet the learning needs of the children. Remember, just because you have planned a particular learning activity, it does not necessarily mean that the children will learn from it what you had expected.

At the end of every day (or session if you operate a separate morning and afternoon nursery), you should review, as a team, which learning activities the children engaged in, which resources were particularly popular and how they were used and go on to consider the impact on future plans: do you, for instance, need to provide more of the same, or do you need to introduce the children to a new piece of equipment or skill?

Remember, plans are there to serve your needs. They should not be written and forgotten about. They should be a working document. I would expect plans to be scribbled all over or have sticky notes fixed to them. I would be extremely concerned if plans were handed in to me in a pristine state: it means that they haven't been reviewed or reflected upon and certainly have not been used to serve the children's learning needs.

Some suggested formats for planning for the Foundation Stage are provided in Figures 4.8 and 4.9.

FOUNDATION STAGE – TERMLY OVERVIEW

AREA OF LEARNING	Date	Date	Date	Date	Date	Date	Date	Date
Personal and social development								
Language and literacy								
Mathematics								
Knowledge and understanding of the world								
Physical development								
Creative development								
Notes								

Figure 4.8 Termly overview

FOUNDATION STAGE – DAILY PLANNING

	Why is activity planned? CI = child initiated (which children) AI = adult initiated AF = adult focus					
	ACTIVITIES					
MONDAY						
	POSSIBLE LEARNING OBJECTIVES					
	Evaluation – where did it lead, resources issues, did focus children engage, how? Add observations made					
	ACTIVITIES					
TUESDAY						
	POSSIBLE LEARNING OBJECTIVES					
	Evaluation					
	ACTIVITIES					
WEDNESDAY						
	POSSIBLE LEARNING OBJECTIVES					
	Evaluation					
	ACTIVITIES					
THURSDAY						
	POSSIBLE LEARNING OBJECTIVES					
	Evaluation					
	ACTIVITIES					
FRIDAY						
	POSSIBLE LEARNING OBJECTIVES					
	Evaluation					
Any other information, issues, etc. that need to be carried forward to next week's planning or recorded in children's individual learning profiles:						

Figure 4.9 Daily planning

What does a learning day look like?

Figure 4.10 illustrates what a learning day in the nursery might look like, while Figure 4.11 gives a typical day in a reception class.

Some days will be different because:

- you have access to a larger learning space for a set period of time, e.g. the school hall;
- you go out in small groups to explore the neighbourhood around your school;
- you go on a class outing;
- you have a visiting expert to your school (this could be one of your parents who has come to talk about their job or their religion or has come to share a skill with the children, an artist in residence, a theatre-in-education group, etc.);
- you are going on a visit to a place of interest, e.g. farm, shops, art gallery, museum, theatre, library;
- the school photographer, school nurse or dentist is visiting; or
- you are having a special day, e.g. dressing up for Book Week or celebrating a religious festival.

The important thing to remember is that every day should be full of exciting learning opportunities. Children can be given the opportunity to join in whole-school activities, too. Some children will want to join a whole-school assembly,

Time	The children	The staff
9.00 or 12.45	• Arrive and start to play	• One member of staff is tasked to liaise with parents • Other staff welcome the children
9.15 or 1.00	• Group time to discuss their learning plans for the session	• One member of staff leads the group session • Other staff talk with individuals who are not comfortable to join the group session
9.20 or 1.05	• Learning individually or in groups • Independently accessing and using resources • Independently accessing fruit and drink	• One member of staff is tasked to observe learning – either focus child/ren or focus activity • Other staff play alongside children, one indoors, one outdoors
11.00 or 2.45	• Tidying up	• Tidying up
11.10 or 2.55	• Group time to discuss their learning	• One member of staff leads the group session • Other staff talk with individuals who are not comfortable to join the group session or finish off the tidying up
11.30 or 3.15	• Staying in the group until a parent comes in to collect them	• One member of staff stays with the group • One member of staff stays by the external door to ensure that no child leaves without an adult

Figure 4.10 How a nursery's learning day might look

Time	The children	The staff
9.00	• Group time to plan for the day, take the register, share news, etc.	• One member of staff is tasked to stay by the door, welcoming the children and parents • One member of staff leads the group session
9.20	• Attend assembly (if they wish)	• One member of staff goes to assembly with children • One member of staff remains in the classroom
9.30	• Engaged in learning activities • Learning individually or in groups • Independently accessing and using resources • Independently accessing fruit and drink	• One adult works indoors • One adult works outdoors • Observations on focus child/ren or focus activities
12.00	• Having lunch and joining in playtime	
1.15	• Back to class • Same pattern as morning	
3.00	• On carpet ready for group time – review of the learning day or a story or singing	• One member of staff leads the group session • Another member of staff completes the tidying up
3.15	• Getting ready to go home or to after-school club	• One member of staff stays with the group • Another member of staff is by the door to ensure that no children go home without an adult

Figure 4.11 How a reception class's learning day might look

particularly if they have a sibling who is taking part. One member of staff could attend assembly and offer the children the opportunity to join her.

Some children may also want to join their siblings for playtimes, too. At the end of playtime, their older sibling can return them to their classroom.

Summary

In this chapter we have looked at personalising learning in the Foundation Stage. We have considered:

● the transition between home and school;
● how you get to know your learners;
● continuing the relationship with parents and carers;
● the learning environment;
● classroom provision;
● the curriculum;
● provision of learning activities;
● observation of learning;
● record keeping;
● planning; and
● what a learning day may look like.

And don't forget to **review** your current practice; decide how you need to **modify it** in order to implement personalising learning.

Transition to Key Stage 1

You will need to consider how you are going to prepare and support the children for the transition from Foundation Stage to Key Stage 1. There is the potential for a huge shift in the learning environment and the ways that learning is facilitated with the introduction of the National Curriculum at the beginning of Key Stage 1, so this transition needs to be carefully thought through and planned.

Your approach to learning needs to be understood by *all* staff in the school and the expectation should be that the children will be continuing to develop as independent, individual learners and that the learning opportunities provided in Key Stage 1 will build on those provided in the Foundation Stage.

Most schools have considered this important transition and build in opportunities towards the end of the term – before the children transfer – for them to visit their new classroom and get to know their new teachers. This can be done with minimum disruption by swapping classes for story time or other learning sessions on a regular basis – perhaps once or twice a week. If staff are new to the school and not available to do this swapping, it is advisable that you arrange for them to visit for at least one day so that they can get to know their class (and their parents at the end of the day) and vice versa.

Another approach is to provide support for the children in the first days and weeks of their transfer. This can be facilitated by the teaching assistants transferring to Year 1 with the children for an initial period. The children will be reassured by seeing a familiar face and the teaching assistant will be an invaluable resource to the new class teacher in terms of her knowledge about the children.

Transfer of information

One aspect of transition that is vital is the transfer of information both from the Foundation Stage and from the parents or carers. An overarching principle of personalising learning is that you are building on what children already know, so the passing on of knowledge about individual learners is crucial.

At the end of the Foundation Stage, the reception class teachers will have completed the Foundation Stage profile for each child. This provides extremely detailed information about the stages of development for each child in each of the early-learning goals (ELGs), but is an unwieldy pile of documents, particularly if you have a class of thirty, to read and inwardly digest.

I would recommend that you adopt the practice of having the Foundation Stage teachers provide a summary document that contains information about the whole class. This form of record keeping for the transfer of information enables the receiving teacher to see at a glance where there are 'gaps' in her learners' development and she can make appropriate provision in the first few days and weeks of the new term. She will have the full profiles to access if she feels the need to look at additional detail.

Figure 5.1 can be used at the end of the reception year. Each child would be recorded in each of the six areas at their achievement level (best fit). A more in-depth summary sheet could be used, if preferred, that provides information against each of the thirteen strands. See Figure 5.2.

You can use the following scale to assist you in completing both of these grids:

- working towards = 1 to 5 scale points achieved
- working around = 6 to 8 scale points achieved
- working beyond = 9 scale points

Name of Class: Date:

	Personal, social and emotional development	Communication, language and literacy	Mathematical development	Knowledge and understanding of the world	Physical development	Creative development
Working towards the ELGs						
Working around the level of ELGs						
Working beyond the ELGs						

Figure 5.1 Summary of children's achievements against the ELGs

Name of class: Date:

	Working towards the ELGs	Working within the ELGs	Met and beyond the ELGs
Disposition and attitudes			
Social development			
Emotional development			
Language for communication and thinking			
Linking sounds and letters			
Reading			
Writing			
Numbers as labels and for counting			
Calculating			
Shape, space and measures			
Knowledge and understanding of the world			
Physical development			
Creative development			

Figure 5.2 Summary of children's achievements against 13 strands of ELGs

While these record sheets give you a snapshot of the learners at the end of the previous term, they do not provide you with the richness of understanding that the previous teacher holds about each learner, nor do they allow for the child's growth and development over the long summer holiday.

Foundation Stage teachers and support staff will have started a detailed learning profile for each child and these should be passed up to the Year 1 teachers, accompanied by a discussion to share this information. Perhaps PPA (planning, preparation and assessment) time could be rearranged to allow these visits to occur during the school day, as they are important professional discussions.

Getting to know your learners

As in the Foundation Stage, you should begin Year 1 by spending as much time as possible observing the children at their play and learning. Your observations of the way they like to work, and with whom, will help you to structure groups for the introduction of more formalised group learning, as well as suggesting learning activities to move the children on in their skill development.

A similar format to classroom observations in the Foundation Stage can be adopted and the same process of discussion at the end of the day of the key learning points for staff from their observations should be maintained, particularly in the early weeks of Year 1, when you are trying to get to know your learners as thoroughly but as quickly as possible. Information can then be transferred to each child's learning profile at regular intervals.

Continuing the relationship with parents

Remember, the parents or carers of the child are the people who still know them best and have watched them develop over the holiday period, so you want to access this information from them as soon as possible into the new term.

Meeting the parents formally

This would usually be facilitated through the setting up of a formal parent–teacher consultation evening. Most schools have consultation evenings in the autumn term but many leave them until just before or just after the half-term holiday (which can be as much as six weeks or longer into the new school year). I would suggest that this is far too long a period to wait for this sharing of knowledge, so the parents' evening would need to be organised to take place within the first three or four weeks of term. This gives the new class teacher time to get to know her new pupils but is not too long before making links with the parents.

The focus for the discussion can be the Foundation Stage profile, because parents should have received information on this at the end of the Foundation Stage. Discussion then moves into the area of how they have seen their children develop over the summer. You will want to hear about:

- their child's attitude and approach to learning;
- what their child likes learning best;
- things their child is good at;
- things their child needs further development in; and
- ways they already help their child with learning at home.

Meeting the parents informally

There will be opportunities to meet with the parents informally at the beginning and end of every day, as they bring or collect their child to or from the classroom. As in the Foundation Stage, it would be good practice to ensure that one adult be designated to liaise with the parents in the mornings while the other adult greets and settles the children.

This liaison role should be rotated so that parents get to know both the teacher and the teaching assistant well and feel equally comfortable speaking to either.

Keeping parents informed

Another simple way to engage parents in the learning of their child is to keep them fully informed about the learning that is happening in school. This can be done simply, by displaying topic plans for the half-term in a place that is accessible to parents as they wait to collect their child from school.

What about parents who are not the people who collect their child from school. How do you keep them informed? One simple way is to provide a topic information sheet such as that in Figure 5.3.

Class:
Your child's topic for this half-term is:

The class will be concentrating on the themes/concepts of:

The maths focus is:

Please send in resources of:

Other relevant information:

(this section could include information such as PE days, planned events and visits)

Figure 5.3 A typical topic information sheet

This sheet would need to be sent home with every child at the beginning of each topic. It can be followed up with year group meetings for parents, in order to brief them about particular aspects of learning for that topic. If you have more than one class per year group, you can run this meeting for the whole year group of parents, enabling staff to share the input. It also reinforces for the parents that whichever class their child is in they will be having access to the same curriculum and learning experiences because staff work together on their planning and delivery.

We found that these meetings were best attended if they were held either first thing in the morning as parents dropped their children off for school or last thing in the afternoon before children were collected, and were best led by the class teachers in a hall space. The children can then remain in their own classroom and continue with their learning during this time.

Learning environment

The environment should be very similar to that of the Foundation Stage classroom. The children still need:

- to feel safe, secure and valued as an individual;
- to know where everything is and how to use it safely;
- to have the space and time maximised for learning;
- to know that the Golden Rules still apply; and
- to have good role models around them.

In order for the children to continue to develop as confident, independent learners, they need to operate in an environment that supports that development and builds on what they have known in their previous learning environments.

Read the section 'Learning environment' in Chapter 4 (pages 35–40) on creating the right environment for PL, and consider the following questions:

CHECKLIST

- Does the emotional environment in your classroom support the continued development of positive self-esteem?
- Is space for learning maximised in the physical environment, both indoors and outdoors?
- Are children enabled to meet their physical needs in your classroom?
- Are classroom routines minimised to ensure that time for learning is maximised?
- Does your classroom environment enable the children to continue to develop as independent learners?

Classroom routines

In addition to the classroom routines discussed in Chapter 4, look also at routines that are new in Key Stage 1, to ensure that time is maximised for learning. Consider routines such as lining the children up, dressing and undressing for PE and playtimes to see if there are alternatives that would save valuable time that can then be used for learning.

For health-and-safety reasons, the children need to learn how to move around the school in an orderly fashion, but I have seen some teachers waste endless minutes waiting for a quiet, straight line before they will leave the classroom. The longer they wait, the more restless the children become, and the longer it takes to get a quiet, straight line.

The trick is to give the children an adequate – maybe a two-minute – warning that you will be leaving the classroom as a whole-class group, and ask them to ensure that they are ready. When it is time to leave, ask the children to go to the door and leave straightaway. If there are two adults in each classroom, one can stay behind to round up any stragglers.

So as not to waste time while the children are dressing and undressing for PE, get them to chant their alphabet or their times tables. Or use the time to talk about what they did last time in PE (review) and what you are going to do in your PE lesson this time, giving them the learning objective so that they can become active as soon as they enter the working space. This gives them time to think about quality in PE before they get to the hall.

Our children complained about set playtimes interfering with their learning time. They would often be in the middle of a task and it would be time to go out to play. They asked if we could move to having flexible playtimes, so that they could go out to play whenever it fitted into their learning agenda for that particular day. Some days playtime would be early, some days late, and some days they might not go out to play at all. Staff agreed to trial this approach to playtimes for one term (that was five years ago and the school still does not have set playtimes).

Because there were always at least two adults in each classroom, one adult could take the children out to play while the other had a comfort break or prepared the classroom for the next learning session. Staff ensured that they took it in turns to go out to play with the children, though sometimes they would both choose to go out. If there was more than one class at play in the playground at any one time, staff could negotiate with each other as to who stayed out, though most chose to stay out with their own class and would get involved in playing games with the children.

When I have spoken to teachers about this approach they have been concerned about staff not being able to get a hot drink or use the toilet. All of our staff purchased safety cups so that they could have hot drinks in the classroom or playground without any danger to the children; and, because of the staffing ratios, adults could use the toilet as and when they needed to, just as the children could.

Classroom provision and use of resources

You will need to consider:

- adult–pupil ratio;
- the type of resources to provide;
- the storage of resources; and
- the use of display.

Maintaining standards in classroom provision and the level of resourcing is vital to ensure continuity in learning. If children feel confident in their learning environment, it follows that their learning will be enhanced. Staffing levels should be maintained wherever possible, so that the children can have their needs met. The environment should support their development as independent learners. Resources and materials should be familiar to them. If they recognise certain resources, they will be confident in their use. New provision and resources can then be added gradually, to allow the children to continue to develop their skills.

Adult–pupil ratio

As in the Foundation Stage, you need to maximise the number of learning facilitators available to the children in their classroom. Most classrooms now have at least two adults, for part if not all of the time, with the teacher and teaching assistant, but it is possible to supplement this figure with trained parent helpers or students in training. As before, anyone supporting learning in your classrooms will need to have a basic understanding of how your school operates and how they can best facilitate learning.

Materials and resources

Staff, in conjunction with the children, will need to organise their classroom to meet their needs. Discuss with the children where they would like their resources kept – guiding them to ensure that logic is applied to their decision making – for example, the resources for messy or wet activities need to be stored near the sink so that they can be easily cleared up.

Resources will still need to be stored in low, accessible places so that the children can be independent in using them and tidying them away. Labelling of drawers and boxes is still a good idea but there should be more written labels around the classroom in Key Stage 1. Why not get the children to make the labels for the drawers and boxes (it gives their writing a real purpose)?

As in the Foundation Stage, a full selection of play activities and resources should be made available so that the children have the opportunity to exercise real choice about their learning. Remember to think about the possible uses of resources when you are purchasing for your classroom. Try to buy resources and equipment that can be used in a variety of ways, in order to stimulate creativity and the use of imagination. A similar selection of natural resources that were provided in the Foundation Stage are still relevant in Key Stage 1 classrooms.

In Key Stage 1, as well as the full selection of play activities and resources, you will need to start introducing the children to resources that will help them with their development in the more formal aspects of learning. Particularly useful are number and alphabet fans. The children can make their own at the beginning of the year – laminated sheets are the best so that they last longer. If you provide the sheet with the fans printed with the numbers and alphabet, then the children can cut them out, order them and join them with a paper fastener. Some children may prefer to work in a linear fashion and will therefore want a number line and alphabet line as well as fans.

The fans can be used during PULSE learning sessions as an assessment tool, with children holding up the correct letter that corresponds to the letter sound that you have just made, or the answer to the number bond that you have just given them. Individual whiteboards and markers can be used during these group sessions to the same effect.

Display

Children in Key Stage 1 should be enabled to contribute to the planning of displays in their classroom. This can be facilitated through discussion at group times or circle time. Ask the children for ideas for display, in terms of the type of work they would like to see displayed and what they think the display should look like.

They could even be involved in beginning to learn how to prepare their work for display. They will need to be taught to use a paper strimmer safely and accurately so that they can mount their own work, and they could use their ICT capabilities to make captions and banners to accompany their work.

As before, all the work displayed should be that of the children. It would also help the children and visitors to the classroom if aspects of the process of their learning could be displayed alongside the finished pieces of work. This can take the form of photographs or captions, explaining how the work was done and the sort of learning that was involved. Perhaps even display some of the evaluative comments the children make about their own or others' work.

CHECKLIST

Revisit the classroom provision checklist in Chapter 4, and ask further:

- Are children enabled to make decisions about the layout of their class-room?
- Are the children being involved in decision making about what should be displayed?
- Are the children being involved in the preparation of their work for display?
- Are children expected to be responsible for their learning environment?

Review your classroom provision.
What changes do you need to introduce so that your classroom provision facilitates personalising learning?

Curriculum

Key Stage 1 sees the introduction of the statutory programmes of study encapsulated by the National Curriculum, which was introduced in 1989 by the government, who were concerned about inequity and inconsistency in the education system. You will need to consider how the introduction of the National Curriculum at this stage will be allowed to impact on your developing personalising learning curriculum.

The National Curriculum raises some interesting issues when it comes to considering personalising learning. It is a statutory duty to deliver the programmes of study for all subjects and RE, but modes of delivery are not stipulated. Recently, following the publication of the DfES document 'Excellence and Enjoyment', schools have been encouraged to be more creative with their curriculum in order to address the learning needs of their pupils.

I would suggest that one of the first questions you should be asking yourselves is, 'Do we have to deliver the National Curriculum in subjects as part of a secondary-school-type timetabled curriculum?'. Your considered response should be that a subject timetable does not fit into the model of personalising learning in the primary school.

So how do you ensure that you are covering the statutory programmes of study, if you are not delivering in timetabled subjects?

Use the National Curriculum as part of your PL curriculum

The National Curriculum can be used as part of your PL curriculum, provided you do not let it skew the curriculum you are developing to match the learning needs of your pupils. You will need to ensure that it is given the appropriate weighting and put in the appropriate place in your curriculum.

Your PL curriculum will need to have the physical, social and emotional needs of the children at its core, including their development as 'good citizens', supported by the development of the skills for lifelong learning. I would suggest that these should be the key elements of personalising learning.

The children should have input into the design of the content of their curriculum (which is where the programmes of study from the National Curriculum will sit) in order to build on their previous knowledge and understanding.

Children who are visual, auditory or kinaesthetic learners should have their learning facilitated through the use of multisensory methods in order to ensure maximum coverage.

The curriculum should be enriched with a range of key entitlements. These entitlements ensure that every child has the opportunity to experience these things on an annual basis as part of their learning programme (see 'Key experiences section, pages 23–4).

You can then go on to consider working towards extended provision by looking at out-of-hours learning. This relies heavily on the goodwill and expertise of individual members of staff, though with the move to 'extended school' status some staff can be employed to run wraparound childcare before and after school.

We took the decision to offer out-of-school activities to all pupils who wanted to be engaged in them from Year 1 upwards. Clubs that were provided were: art, games, football, hockey, netball, chess, computers, guitar, dance, recorder, cheer-leading and gymnastics. The clubs that you can offer will depend on the interests of your staff and their willingness to see the importance of their engagement in these worthwhile activities.

With these four aspects in place, your PL curriculum would look something like Figure 5.4.

The core of your curriculum would be PSHE, including the development of citizenship and learning skills. Table 5.1 gives an example of a core curriculum for Key Stage 1.

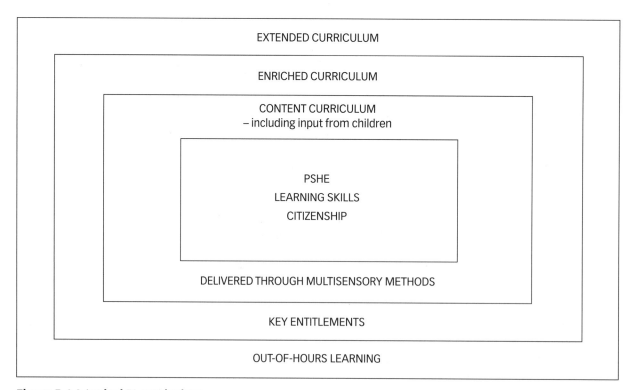

Figure 5.4 A typical PL curriculum

SKILLS	KNOWLEDGE AND UNDERSTANDING
Independence and responsibility Assertiveness Self-esteem Feelings	• Develop the ability to set own goals, both academically and socially • Gain confidence in managing social situations • Develop an ability to present themselves positively to others. • Develop an awareness of a variety of emotions and discuss the management of these.
Respect for people, environment and property	• Develop the ability to speak other languages • Develop an understanding of different cultures/religions • Understand the need for sustainable use of resources • Understand and upkeep the Golden Rules
Personal management/healthy lifestyle	• Be responsible/independent for own personal hygiene/safety in and out of school • Develop an understanding of a healthy diet and the benefits of regular exercise • Be given opportunities to experience a variety of physical exercise and be encouraged to participate by choice in extracurricular activities.
Self-assessment and evaluation of learning	• Develop the vocabulary needed to express learning needs, strengths and areas for further development • Personal Effectiveness Programme Initiative (PEPI) skills assessment (see later in this chapter)
Managing relationships in a variety of contexts	• Understand and develop respect for others feelings, decisions, rights, etc. • Understand the need for and develop the language of mediation • Know that some activities are best undertaken by groups and be given opportunities to work in a variety of group situations
Effective communication	• Be able to speak and listen in small and large groups appropriately • Understand the value of different forms of communication • Value and evaluate different points of view • Develop the confidence to offer own views and ideas
Problem solving	• Develop an awareness of a problem having more than one solution • Develop the ability to generate a plan, implement and evaluate it • Begin to develop an ability to problem-solve within a group
Research skills	• Be able to use the library and begin to develop reference skills • Begin to develop an understanding of what research is and how it can benefit learning
Thinking skills	• Begin to understand the process of learning • Begin to develop an understanding of the difference between facts, bias and opinion • Make value judgements about what they are reading

Table 5.1 An example of a core curriculum for Key Stage 1

For the content curriculum, you will need to define the skills and aptitudes needed for each subject area. You can then either plan the children's learning around the key skills from each subject discipline in a cohesive, cross-curricular way or you can retain discrete subjects as part of your curriculum plan. There follows an example of suggested key skills, listed by subject discipline (you will notice that a lot of the key skills are common across many disciplines).

Literacy

- Develop positive attitudes to literacy.
- Develop a range of communication skills through a wide range of experiences:
  - reflective listening;
  - speaking clearly, coherently and confidently;
  - constructing and sustaining a logical argument;
  - starting, engaging in and maintaining a conversation;
  - reading with fluency, accuracy and understanding of meaning;
  - understanding the differences in the presentation by writers of fact and fiction and learning to use the organisational features of texts;
  - developing an understanding of a variety of genres in their reading and writing; and
  - developing the skills of planning, drafting, editing and presentation in their writing.
- Develop speaking and listening, reading and writing skills in a range of purposeful contexts.
- Develop a sense of audience for their literacy work.

Numeracy

- Develop positive attitudes to numeracy.
- Develop a range of mathematical skills through a wide range of experiences:
  - understanding the number system and using it accurately and appropriately;
  - developing a range of strategies for number operations and using them accurately and appropriately in both mental and written calculations;
  - developing an understanding of pattern and the properties of shape, space and measures; and
  - developing data-handling skills, including the representation and interpretation of data.
- Develop confidence in mental mathematics and the use of a range of mathematical strategies and tools in a range of purposeful contexts.
- Develop the ability to communicate their mathematics to a variety of audiences.

Science

- Develop positive attitude to science.
- Develop a range of scientific skills and strategies through a wide range of experiences and purposeful contexts:
  - understanding the importance of evidence gathering and presentation in scientific enquiry;
  - developing investigative skills; and
  - developing the skills of evaluation.

- Develop the ability to communicate their scientific work to a variety of audiences.

ICT

- Develop positive attitudes to ICT.
- Develop a range of ICT skills and strategies through a wide range of experiences and purposeful contexts:
  - developing the skills to use a range of ICT equipment;
  - developing the skills to record, store and retrieve information from a range of ICT equipment; and
  - understanding the uses of ICT in their world.
- Develop the ability to communicate through ICT to a variety of audiences.

History

- Develop positive attitudes to history.
- Develop a range of historical skills and strategies through a wide range of experiences and purposeful contexts:
  - distinguishing between fact and fiction;
  - appreciating that an event can be seen from different perspectives;
  - developing chronological skills;
  - developing a questioning approach to any form of evidence, including primary and secondary sources; and
  - developing the ability to locate, select and organise historical information.
- Develop the ability to communicate historical findings to a range of audiences.

Geography

- Develop positive attitudes to geography.
- Develop a range of geographical skills and strategies through a wide range of experiences and purposeful contexts:
  - developing a geographical vocabulary;
  - developing the powers of observation;
  - developing an awareness of how people have changed places and how places affect people;
  - developing an understanding of the physical features and systems of the earth;
  - developing a questioning approach to any form of evidence, including primary and secondary sources;
  - developing an understanding and interest in environmental issues;
  - developing the ability to use accurately, a variety of resources (maps, globes, newspaper, written texts, video, etc.); and
  - developing the ability to communicate their geographical knowledge to a variety of audiences.

Art

- Develop positive attitudes to art.
- Develop a range of art skills and strategies through a wide range of experiences and purposeful contexts:
  - experimenting and exploring with a variety of resources, materials and techniques, learning to use each when most appropriate;

    – developing, extending and sequencing work over time;
    – recording what has been observed, remembered and imagined in two- and three-dimensional work; and
    – developing the skills of art appreciation.
- Develop the ability to communicate art knowledge, skill and ability to a variety of audiences.

Design and technology

- Develop positive attitudes to design and technology.
- Develop a range of skills and strategies in design and technology through a wide range of experiences and purposeful contexts:
    – showing curiosity in the investigation of different materials, and using and extending knowledge about materials as they design and make products;
    – developing a range of techniques and processes for working creatively with materials; and
    – developing the skills of planning, organising, making and evaluating their products.
- Develop the ability to communicate design and technology knowledge, skill and ability to a variety of audiences.

Music

- Develop positive attitudes to music.
- Develop a range of skills and strategies in music through a wide range of experiences and purposeful contexts:
    – developing reflective listening in order to respond to musical elements, mood and the character of music;
    – developing the capacity to express ideas and emotions through music;
    – using and understanding simple signs and symbols for musical sounds;
    – imitating and recalling simple rhythms and melodies;
    – developing the skills needed to control the sounds of a range of instruments, including voice;
    – creating and organising sounds in response to different stimuli and being prepared to practise, rehearse and respond to direction in order to take part in vocal and instrumental improvisations and compositions; and
    – developing the skills of assessing and evaluating own work and the work of others.
- Develop the ability to communicate music knowledge, skill and ability to a variety of audiences.

Physical education

- Develop positive attitudes to PE.
- Develop a range of skills and strategies in PE through a wide range of experiences and purposeful contexts:
    – developing flexibility, strength and endurance;
    – developing good posture and the correct use of the body at all times, to ensure safety;
    – developing skills through practice and repetition;
    – developing the understanding of the effects of regular physical exercise on the body;

- observing conventions of fair play, honest competition and good sporting behaviour;
  - developing the skills of evaluation of own performance and that of others; and
  - lifting, carrying and placing equipment correctly and safely.
- Develop the ability to communicate PE knowledge, skill and ability to a variety of audiences.

Religious education

- Develop positive attitudes to RE.
- Develop a range of skills and strategies in RE through a wide range of experiences and purposeful contexts:
  - developing knowledge about the diversity of the main religious beliefs of the world and the range of issues this raises;
  - developing understanding of the use of religious concepts and symbols;
  - distinguishing between various literary forms as they are used in different religions;
  - exercising critical and appreciative judgement in order to distinguish between prejudice, superstition and opinion; and
  - developing an understanding of the experiences, intentions, beliefs and desires of other people.
- Develop the ability to communicate RE knowledge, skill and ability to a variety of audiences.

As staff and governors, we also decided that we wanted to include a modern foreign language in our curriculum. French was introduced from Year 1 with some vocabulary being introduced in nursery and reception classes.

If you prefer not to consider curriculum content in terms of separate timetabled subjects, then I suggest you look at the nine areas of learning and experience devised by HMI in 1985. My staff and I found that these areas fitted more easily with our approach to learning. In their document, 'The Curriculum from 5 to 16', HMI state (on p. 9),

> There are limitations in a curriculum which is no more than a list of subjects. For example, it is too easy to define the content of each subject with no reference whatever to the learning processes to be used or what is happening in the rest of the curriculum.

The paper was written to stimulate the professional discussion about the whole curriculum. It was HMI's attempt at providing a framework for curriculum planning, to ensure a broad, balanced, relevant and coherent curriculum.

We liked these broad areas and their definitions because it made links across subjects and seemed to reflect the real world much better than the National Curriculum. The areas they defined were as follows.

Aesthetic and creative: The capacity to respond emotionally and intellectually to sensory experience; the awareness of degrees of quality; the appreciation of beauty and fitness for purpose; the exploration and understanding of feeling and the processes of making, composing and inventing.

Human and social: Understanding people and how they live, their relationships with each other and with their environments, and how human action, now and in the past, has influenced events and conditions. The significance of place and its effects on the natural and created world – this area includes historical, geographical, technological, political and sociological perspectives; the study and preservation of environments. Understanding of how economic systems work, and the way in which costs and benefits to society and to the individual must be evaluated when making choices about the use of scarce human, financial and material resources.

Linguistic and literary: Increasing pupils' understanding of the role and power of language in all aspects of life, their confidence as language users and their enjoyment of a wide variety of literary and other texts from a range of sources and cultures.

Mathematical: Developing mathematical concepts and processes to enable pupils to understand and appreciate relationships and patterns in both number and space in their everyday lives and be able to express them clearly and concisely.

Moral: Bringing together moral actions and the principles that underline them; providing experiences that help to form and test moral convictions and to modify attitudes; providing opportunities to reason about values if people are to make sound moral judgements. Moral aspects of personal and social development.

Physical: Those activities that normally belong within the field of physical education and dance that aim to develop control, coordination and mobility and to provide for the development of knowledge, understanding and attitudes. Manipulative and motor skills and knowledge of how the human body works, the development of a healthy attitude towards it and adoption of an active way of life to keep it in good condition.

Scientific: Increasing pupils' knowledge and understanding of the natural world, the world as modified by human beings and with developing skills and competences associated with science as a process of enquiry. These include: observation, selection, hypothesising, experimentation and communication.

Spiritual: Developing feelings and convictions about the significance of human life and the world as a whole; religious education is contained within this area but is not identical with it.

Technological: The search for ways and means to extend and enhance our powers to control events and order our environment. The essence for technology lies in process of bringing about change or exercising control over the environment. This process is a particular form of problem solving, of designing in order to effect control.

Getting ready to learn

Learning is a serious business and the children need to be receptive to it. We have earlier thought about the learning environment and how conducive it is to learning, ensuring that the children have enough time and space for learning and that their physical needs are met; but, if they are not emotionally and mentally ready for learning, it can be a waste of time and energy. There follow some ideas to aid children in achieving the right mental state for learning, i.e. calm and focused.

Yoga

Simple yoga exercises can be introduced to the children as a way of developing good posture, focus and concentration. Initially, an adult would lead the yoga session but, as children become more confident and learned appropriate technique and a range of positions, they could be asked to lead sessions. A good resource to use is 'Yoga for Children' cards (Buckley, 2003).

The children should be led calmly and slowly through a selection of the exercises, introducing some of the basic postures and positions first and gradually introducing the more complicated movements as the children make progress. Music can be used to help create a calm atmosphere.

You should discuss the principles of yoga with the children so that they understand that the exercises are designed to help them be better learners by helping them to have good posture, good breathing techniques and a healthy body.

You do not need to have long yoga sessions to see the benefits: an odd five- or ten-minute session can be extremely beneficial, particularly at the beginning of learning sessions following a playtime.

Brain Gym®

As well as yoga, you can also use brain-gym activities to enable the children to be ready for learning and keep them focused for learning. Below are some good exercises for Key Stage 1 children.

Brain buttons

By rubbing the 'brain buttons', we stimulate the neurological pathways related to the two sides of the brain working together. You'll find your brain buttons at the soft spots under your collarbone. Rub them with the thumb and first finger of one hand. Cover your belly button with the first finger and middle finger of your other hand.

You can also rest your tongue on the roof of your mouth and think pleasant thoughts. After a minute of this exercise, you'll feel refreshed and ready for anything!

Cross-lateral working

This can be any form of cross-crawl movement. It stimulates both sides of the brain at once, increasing learning capability.

- Raise your left knee and touch it with the opposite hand. Alternate knees and hands.
- Touch your knee with your elbow. Alternate knees and elbows.
- Kick out one leg and the opposite arm. Alternate legs and arms.

Do your cross-crawl exercises to a variety of music and rhythms.

Thinking cap

This stimulates the reflex points that enhance hearing and understanding.

Using your thumbs and first fingers, slowly pull the edges of your ears out and backwards. Start at the top and work down to your earlobes. Repeat this two or three times.

Positive points

This brings circulation to the front of the brain, helping to balance the emotional stress with a rational attitude.

Your positive points are on your forehead, between your eyebrows and your hairline. They may feel like two small bumps. Hold them when something is worrying you. Do this for one minute or until you feel better.

Lazy 8s

The Lazy 8 is an easy way to learn to smoothly cross the visual midline that connects the left and right visual fields. It will help improve the sense of balance and coordination and promote the ability to write without stress.

Lay your ear on your shoulder and reach out your arm from your nose (a bit like an elephant's trunk). Swing your arm, your head, and the top half of your body through the air, as if you're drawing a figure 8 lying on its side. Do this two or three times. When you feel ready, follow your finger with your eyes as it draws.

Developing learning behaviours in children

At the beginning of every focused group learning session, introduce the learning objective. One way of doing this is to have it written on the board in the room and ask the children to read it out. Many teachers make learning-objective posters and laminate them so they can be written on for every session. Others get children to ask the question, 'What are we going to learn next?' at the start of a session. It doesn't matter how you share the learning objective with the children as long as you do. The children should then be asked what the learning objective means in order to ensure that they have understood what is expected of them.

Success criteria should then be discussed. This can be done in terms of 'What will a good piece of work look like for this session?'. If you do this exercise at the beginning of every session, the children will be developing a deep understanding of what constitutes quality in many and varied possible learning outcomes, whether it be in the form of a piece of writing, a learning poster, a model, a painting, a dance or a musical composition. Get the answers from the children so that during this time you can be assessing their level of understanding of success criteria for this learning activity. The success criteria can be written up as a learning poster and displayed around the classroom so that the children have them to refer to during their working time.

By having these conversations on a regular basis, the children will begin to develop a shared understanding of what constitutes quality learning outcomes in your school and will help to ensure consistency across the school in terms of presentation, etc.

Before sending children off to work, you need to check that they have really understood what is expected of them. To do this you can introduce a system of 'traffic lights'. At the beginning of the school year in Year 1, get the children to make themselves a traffic-light fan, consisting of a red, amber and green strip of card, joined at the bottom by a paper fastener. (If the strips are laminated, they will last much longer.) The traffic lights can then be used as part of every introductory session to check the level of understanding. After a session of direct teaching, the children are asked to show 'green' if they have understood what has been spoken about, 'amber' if they are not 100 per cent sure and 'red' if they need to have it explained to them again. The 'green' children can be sent off to work straightaway, the 'amber' children can be asked to sit themselves close to a 'green' child and use them as a reference and the 'red' children can remain for further explanation or practical demonstration or become a group that the adult would work closely with for that session – a focus group.

This method can also be used after instructions have been given. 'Green' would be shown if the children knew exactly what to do; 'amber' if they needed some guidance or support (ask them to sit next to a 'green' person); and 'red' if they feel that they need support from an adult (this is where you sit yourself as the teacher or ask your teaching assistant to support the group).

You will find that over the course of the year, the traffic lights will assist greatly with classroom organisation, as well as assessment. It gives you immediate feedback on where the children think they are in terms of their levels of knowledge and understanding.

CAUTION

- The traffic lights will be only a rough guide, since this is based on the child's perceptions and will need to be confirmed through other means of assessment.
- Some children might use their traffic lights as a way to seek attention, either by over- or underestimating their own abilities – you will soon become aware of those children.

During the plenary at the end of the learning session, the success criteria can be referred to again. Children can be asked to reflect on their own piece of work with regard to the success criteria and make a realistic judgement as to whether they have achieved success this time and what they will need to do to improve next time. This can be done through a quiet thinking time at the beginning of the plenary session. Children can be asked to think quietly for one minute about what they want to say about their piece of work in order to help them to prepare before they are asked to speak. (Far too often, we expect children to give an immediate response without having time to clarify their thoughts.)

You can use traffic lights as part of this plenary session to check the confidence levels of the children in their new learning.

Once they are practised at this self-evaluation, they can be asked to provide feedback to their peers (usually by the spring term in Year 2), using the success criteria to make the feedback specific and worthwhile. This can be managed either through the use of learning partners (see 'Study buddies or learning partners' section, page 28), whereby the children are asked to work in their given pairs to look at each other's work and give feedback; or as a whole-class activity, whereby a child is asked to read out their piece of work and comments are sought from the 'floor'.

Building in choice for children

You will want to maintain and build upon the level of choice that the children exhibited during the Foundation Stage. This can be done in several ways in Key Stage 1.

- In the morning children can be given a list of tasks that need to be completed by the end of the day, and they can choose when to do them and in which order.
- Children can be given open-ended tasks and choose how they would like to represent their learning.
- Children could choose whom to work with on certain learning tasks.
- Children could choose where they would like to learn – indoors or outdoors, at a table or on the floor, etc.
- If you teach in a school with two-form entry or higher, you could operate a system within your team of providing a range of different activities in each classroom and children could choose which classroom they would like to work in for that day or part of a day.

If this level of choice is to be made available to the children, there are obvious consequences for the adults. They will need to be much more flexible and responsive to the children's needs in their approach to facilitating learning.

Remember that the children will need to develop their self-discipline in order to manage this high level of responsibility, so you will need to ensure that there is time available for a lot of discussion around the issues of choice and responsibility – actions and consequences.

But it is only by exercising choice and reflecting on the outcomes of your decisions that you can develop this skill. We need to ensure that our children get plenty of practice in decision making in a safe and supportive school environment before they are making life choices in and about their future.

Learning activities

You will need to consider carefully the types of learning activity that you employ, ensuring that they complement, rather than undermine, your move towards personalising learning. Obviously, you will need to be introducing the children to the more formal aspects of learning at this stage, but this should reflect the child's aptitude and interests rather than be planned for everyone just because they are in Year 1 now.

Developing the five Rs

1 Resilience

Build upon the children's developing abilities to stick at their learning. This can be done by increasing gradually your expectations of them, both in terms of time spent on a piece of learning and in the quantity of work produced.

Use study buddies or learning partners to provide peer feedback on the children's developing resilience as part of your plenary sessions. Provide suitable opportunities for the children to be adventurous in their learning and encourage them to be risk takers. Model being adventurous for them by trying to develop new skills yourself.

Continue to support children in their development of the attitudes and skills needed to deal with difficulties and confusion. Remember that you are not there to sort out their problems for them, thereby making them dependent on you. Encourage them to try to sort out their own difficulties and develop patience in working through their confusion. If there are some children who have developed good ways of dealing with difficulties, use them as 'troubleshooters' to assist others.

Talk to them during group times or circle time about the strategies they use for problem solving and handling confusion. They can learn from each other in this way.

2 Resourcefulness

Build on the levels of independence established for the children in the Foundation Stage and encourage them to continue to look for their own creative approaches to their learning.

Remember, your classroom will need to be well resourced and children will need to be shown how to use resources and equipment safely.

3 Reflectiveness

Encourage the children to continue to think about their learning and their approaches to learning so that they can share their strategies with others.

By Key Stage 1 the children should be building quite a wide vocabulary to describe their learning approaches and their learning needs. They should be able to make effective choices about the way that they approach a new piece of learning and they should be able to ask for assistance if they need to learn a new skill to enable them to complete a task.

4 Remembering

Continue to use a range of techniques and strategies with the children to support their developing memory skills. In Key Stage 1 they should be encouraged to come up with their own techniques and strategies and share them with others.

Use learning posters to aid memory. For example, if you want the children to develop their vocabulary for a particular topic, by learning the names for the parts of a flower, say, have a poster showing a labelled diagram and, in a few spare moments at the ends of sessions during the day, do a quick-fire point-and-shout session. You point to the part and the children shout out the name of the part. Repeat this over a week and the children will soon begin to remember the new vocabulary. You could get the children to make the learning posters for the class as part of their learning activities.

5 Responsiveness

As the children are developing in maturity by this stage, they should be more able to manage change and uncertainty with confidence. They should be displaying this confidence in their approach to new learning and should be able to manage greater levels of insecurity than in the Foundation Stage. This will make it possible for them to work in other classrooms and with a wider range of adults.

Reading resources

In order to support the children in the development of their individual skills as a reader, you will need to consider the resources you provide for them to read. Some schools have a particular reading scheme; others prefer a 'real books' approach.

For PL you will need to cover all the angles and provide as many different resources for reading as possible. Some children will need the framework of a reading scheme; others will flourish from having the flexibility and freedom to choose their own material for reading. Some will learn to read phonetically, others will use a whole-word approach. What you need to provide is a mixed menu so that there will be something that appeals to every palate.

Children should have a high level of freedom of choice when it comes to their reading materials. If they are reading materials that they have chosen, they are more likely to be motivated to read them and therefore will see the importance and relevance of developing the appropriate skills.

Groups for reading

Most class teachers group children by ability for formal learning, such as literacy and numeracy. I would suggest that for PL to be effective children need to work in mixed-ability groups for most, if not all, activities. By working in mixed-ability groups, children have the opportunity to learn from others and share successful strategies. Remember, it is not always the 'clever' children who have the ability to describe the best strategies for learning: sometimes someone who is struggling with a concept or skill will be able to describe their creative approaches and solutions to difficulties in a much more accessible way.

Listening to children read

When you are listening to a child read, you should be focusing on their developing reading skills. You should be noticing (and recording):

- whether the text is known or unknown to the child;
- whether they appear confident or hesitant;
- how involved they are with the text;
- whether, when they 'get stuck' on a word, they:
  - stop and wait to be told;
  - try to sound it out for themselves;
  - guess;
  - guess, using contextual clues or illustrations; or
  - self-correct if the word they say is obviously wrong;
- whether the child liked/enjoyed the book, and why; and
- whether the child can talk about the book after they have read it, and whether they are accessing the meaning from the text or 'barking at the print'.

There is more on keeping reading records later in this chapter.

Writing

Children who have difficulty in developing the correct letter formation may need to have a range of learning opportunities provided before they begin to use pencil and paper.

For example, a boy in Year 1 hated handwriting. He would often refuse to pick up a pencil and had difficulty in remembering letter formations because he did not like to practise. But he was a very active child and particularly liked to work and play outside. His teacher's solution was to put him on a bike and send him outside with a teaching assistant and a piece of chalk. His challenge was to draw the letters as big as he could with the chalk on the playground. Then he was asked to sit on his bike and go the place where the letter started. He was then encouraged to ride his bike around the letter, practising the correct letter formation over and over again. He was then asked to walk and run around the letter formation a few times. When he was later encouraged to write his letters in a sand tray, formulating the letters with a finger in wet sand, the teaching assistant reminded him of his movements outside, to get him to visualise how the letters are formed. This was later translated to paint on paper and finally to pencil on paper.

When the children are developing their skills in the area of written communication, you will need to provide a range of formats to assist them with their planning for writing, e.g. ideas boxes and writing frames.

Ideas boxes are used to support those children who find it difficult to have ideas for their writing. You will need to collect together four boxes of a similar size and label them with:

- who;
- where;
- when; and
- what.

The 'who' box will have cards that have possible characters for stories on one side and possible describing words on the other. The 'where' box will have the same for settings. The 'when' box will have ideas about time frames for stories, e.g. 'long, long ago', 'yesterday', 'one fine morning', etc. The 'what' box will have ideas for plot or things that can happen in a story. (Laminate the cards and then they will last longer.)

You can use a class group session to get the children thinking and talking in partners to generate ideas for the boxes and they can continue to add ideas as they mature as writers.

The children can then use the boxes when they get stuck for ideas. If they are still unable to use the cards to get started, they may need to work with their learning partner or study buddy to chat through their ideas first.

In order to help the children develop the concept that a story has a beginning, a middle and an end, you can introduce simple planning frames for them to use (Figure 5.5 shows an example of a simple planning frame). If the children are not at the stage of being able to write independently with confidence, they can still use the planning frame and draw their story instead of writing it. An adult can then work with them and scribe their story for them.

As the children mature as writers, they can be introduced to more sophisticated planning and writing frames. They can use the frame to plan the outline of their story before they begin – using the frame sheet as an aide memoir, to record good words to use to describe their characters, etc.

Who?	Where?	Beginning	Middle	End

Figure 5. 5 Simple planning frame

By providing a range of writing frames, you are enabling the children to choose a frame that best suits their way of working – some children will prefer to plan in a pictorial form, others by jotting words or phrases, some in a linear form, etc.

The writing frames should be kept as a resource that is accessible to the children as and when they need to use them.

Some examples of writing frames are provided in Figure 5.6

Other children may prefer to plan using a plain piece of paper – devising their own planning pro forma. Remember that the important issue is that the children get to choose their own preferred way of planning for their creative writing.

ICT

Children should be developing the notion that ICT equipment is just another learning tool to be used as and when appropriate for the task in hand. Equipment such as:

- tape recorders;
- video recorders;
- digital cameras;
- computers, including laptops; and
- printers

should be readily available for the children to use as tools in their learning.

As always, they will need to be shown how to use the equipment correctly and learn how to be selective in what they choose to keep as a permanent record of their learning.

Key Stage 1 SATs

Needless to say, you should not let the SATs impact on your approaches to learning. It should not be necessary to abandon 'learning' in order to 'revise' for the SATs. The children will respond positively to the new experience of SATs if they have been prepared in terms of knowing how to approach a new activity with confidence and have a range of strategies available to them, such as knowing to read the question carefully first and think about what is being asked for; knowing to base their answers on the text; to show their thinking processes; to reread and check their answers to be sure that they haven't made any silly mistakes.

A **cartoon strip planning frame**: children would draw pictures in the top frames and write a sentence about the beginning, middle and end of their story in the bottom frames.

Beginning	Middle	End

A who, where, when, what planning sheet:

Who?	Where?	When?	What?

This can also be presented as a vertical planner.

Some children prefer to plan using a mind-map approach:

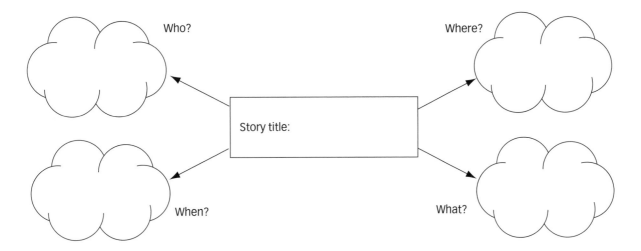

Figure 5.6 Examples of writing frames

We would ensure that, during SATs time, the children would be engaged in lots of practical activities when they were not completing the papers, to try to bring some balance to the learning week and to try to ensure that stress levels were kept low. Staff would not talk about 'tests' but refer to the papers as another new learning activity that they were going to try out with the children to see if they liked it. In all, we did our best to keep it low-key for the children.

Our parents would tell us that their children often did not realise that they were doing the SATs because it was just another new learning experience for them and the children were confident in their approach to new learning. Some children even asked if they could do more of that kind of learning (filling in booklets) because it was something that they had had little experience of in their learning at our school.

Observation of learning

Adults will continue to observe children at their learning, but in Key Stage 1 we should be starting to encourage the children to be self-aware and 'observe' themselves at their learning. By developing their awareness of themselves at their learning, the children will be able to focus on how they learn best, becoming more aware of what works for them.

Self-assessment

It follows that putting the child at the centre of the curriculum and learning that they should also be at the centre of any assessment system too. Children have been used to the 'plan-do-review' discussions in nursery and reception so they are already beginning to form their own judgements about their development as learners. In Year 1 you can introduce a system that engages them in recording their judgements, as long as they can produce evidence to substantiate their claims.

A system that my staff and I devised was based on Gordon Bell's Personal Effectiveness Programme Initiative, or PEPI (1995). He devised the system as a way for his secondary boys to record their achievements in the following key skills:

- presentation skills;
- time-management skills;
- research skills;
- communication skills;
- organisation skills;
- team-working and interpersonal skills; and
- problem-solving and decision-making skills.

We took the programme's key skills and created 'I can' statements that were relevant to children in Key Stage 1.

The children need to be introduced to PEPI. We used a clown puppet to represent him as Bell had used a clown logo on his documentation. PEPI was introduced to the children during an assembly and they were told that PEPI would be very interested in seeing them develop as learners. But PEPI has a very bad memory and wouldn't be able to remember all the children and their achievements, so they would need to write things down for him. He had designed a sheet to help them think about their learning and to show that they were getting better at it as they grew older. The sheet recorded all the 'I can' statements on one side and had a picture of PEPI juggling the skills as balls on the other side. The children could colour the balls as they signed off each target heading.

Either children could choose a target statement to develop or others could point out to them through feedback that they had achieved a target through their everyday learning. The target would then be highlighted by the child, signed and dated by an adult following a discussion with the child as to why they believed that they have achieved the target.

PEPI statements for Key Stage 1

Presentation skills
- I can dress myself smartly
- I can write my name clearly
- I can speak clearly to a group
- I come to school ready to learn
- I always remember to title and date my work
- I can mount my work
- I can speak clearly to a variety of audiences

Time-management skills
- I can listen at carpet time
- I can finish my work on time

Research skills
- I know how to find out things
- I know lots of ways to find out things
- I can sort and use information

Communication skills
- I can talk about something of interest
- I know how someone else is feeling
- I can make my talk interesting

Organisation skills
- I can get what I need for my work
- I can set up my table for work

Team-working and interpersonal skills
- I can share with others
- I can work as part of a group on a piece of work
- I can organise a group

Adults observing learning

It is still a valuable exercise for adults to engage in formally observing the children at their learning and making a record of their observations. You could use the same format as those used in the Foundation Stage to record your observations.

Ensure that the knowledge gained about the individual children's developing approaches to learning are recorded in their learning profile. Remember to provide feedback to the children and their parents on your findings from your observations so that they continue to have an up-to-date picture too.

Record keeping

You need to be sure that you have an up-to-date picture of each child as a learner. There are the day-to-day organisational records, such as those kept for reading, but then there are the records that capture a child's development as a learner.

Maintaining the learning profile

The learning profile kept on each child by the Foundation Stage staff will have been passed up with the child and should be regularly updated (at least twice a term) to ensure up-to-date records are in place for each child. In this way, you will be able to track each child's development over time, and, with regular review of each child's progress, you can highlight children who may need additional support in particular areas or who have a special educational need.

Work sampling

In order to build on the portfolio of learning established in the Foundation Stage, you will need to continue collecting regular samples of work from the children. These can be put together as a portfolio in a scrapbook, culminating in a record of learning development from nursery to Year 6.

Remember that these samples do not have to be only work done on paper. They can be photographs of the child at work, or of their completed work in 3D or video clips if they show their physical or social development. Try to ensure that in the samples you collect you are covering all aspects of the child's development and not just their cognitive development.

It is in line with your working towards PL if the child has input into the decision as to what should be put into their portfolio. They can be asked to choose pieces of work that show that they have improved in aspects of their learning or pieces that they particularly like. The reason for their choice should be recorded as part of the annotation that accompanies the work. An example of an annotation sheet is given as Figure 5.7.

Name: Date:

Who chose the work?

child teacher TA parent (circle as appropriate)

Reason for choice:

Comment:

Figure 5.7 Annotation sheet to accompany work samples

Once completed, the annotation sheet can then be attached to the piece of work or pasted into the child's portfolio in order to provide a context.

Reading records

Reading records should not record only the number of pages read but should give a detailed picture of the child's developing reading skills. One excellent format for reading record keeping is based on the Centre for Language in Primary Education's (CLPE, 1988) becoming-a-reader scale and reading-across-the-curriculum scale. The original scales have been adapted into 'I' statements, thereby making them more personal for the children.

Scale 1 moves from dependence to independence and Scale 2 from inexperienced to experienced (see Tables 5.2 and 5.3). They both give statements of proficiency in a range of reading skills. You can have either a scale sheet for each child, which you would keep with the learning profile and highlight skills as they develop, or one scale sheet that you use as reference and record the children's reading progress in a reading diary.

The benefit of writing the skill development in the reading diary is that the parents would have access to these comments as the diary travels between home and school. Parents should be encouraged to record their observations of their child's development as a reader in the reading diary too. If they are unsure of what to write, you can provide a prompt sheet for them with suggested comments that they might use.

DEPENDENCE	
Beginner reader	• I do not yet have enough successful strategies for tackling print independently. • I rely on having another person read the text aloud. • I may still be unaware that text carries meaning.
Non-fluent reader	• I can tackle known and predictable texts with growing confidence but still need support with new and unfamiliar ones. • I have a growing ability to predict meanings and I am developing strategies to check predictions against other cues such as the illustrations and the print itself.
Moderately fluent reader	• I am well launched on reading but still need to return to a familiar range of texts. • At the same time I am beginning to explore new kinds of texts independently. • I am beginning to read silently.
Fluent reader	• I am a capable reader who now approaches familiar texts with confidence but still needs support with unfamiliar materials. • I am beginning to draw inferences from books and stories that I read independently. • I choose to read silently.
Exceptionally fluent reader	• I am an avid and independent reader who is making choices from a wide range of material. • I am able to appreciate nuances and subtleties in text.
INDEPENDENCE	

Table 5.2 Becoming a reader: scale 1

Here are some suggestions for prompts to assist parents in making comments in the reading diary.

- We talked about the pictures.
- My child could tell me the story by using the pictures. They knew a few words.
- My child joined in with me as I read the story.
- My child read the book correctly but seemed to know it from memory.
- My child read a simple story easily by themselves.
- My child read familiar words correctly but I needed to tell them some unfamiliar words.
- My child found this book hard, so I read it to them.
- I gave clues to certain words but my child guessed correctly without being told.
- My child made a good attempt at sounding out unfamiliar words.

INEXPERIENCED	
Inexperienced reader	• My experience as a reader has been limited. • Generally, I choose to read very easy and familiar texts where illustrations play an important part. • I have difficulty with any unfamiliar material and yet I may be able to read my own dictated texts confidently. • I need a great deal of support with the reading demands of the classroom. • I tend to be overdependent on one strategy when reading aloud, often reading word by word. • I rarely choose to read for pleasure.
Less experienced reader	• I am developing fluency as a reader and reading certain kinds of material with confidence. • I usually choose short books with simple narrative shapes and with illustrations and may read these silently. • I often reread favourite books. • My reading for pleasure often includes comics and magazines. • I need help with the reading demands of the classroom, and especially with using reference and information books.
Moderately experienced reader	• I am a confident reader who feels at home with books. • I generally read silently and I am developing stamina as a reader. • I am able to read for longer periods and cope with more demanding texts, including children's novels. • I am willing to reflect on reading and often use reading in my own learning. • I select books independently and can use information books and materials for straightforward reference purposes, but still need help with unfamiliar material, particularly non-narrative prose.
Experienced reader	• I am a self-motivated, confident and experienced reader who may be pursuing particular interests through reading. • I am capable of tackling some demanding texts and can cope well with the reading of the curriculum. • I read thoughtfully and appreciate shades of meaning. • I am capable of locating and drawing on a variety of sources in order to research a topic independently.
Exceptionally experienced reader	• I am an enthusiastic and reflective reader who has a strong established taste in fiction and/or non-fiction. • I enjoy pursuing my own reading interests independently. • I can handle a wide range and variety of texts, including some adult material. • I recognise that different texts require different styles of reading. • I am able to evaluate evidence drawn from a variety of information sources. • I am developing critical awareness as a reader.
EXPERIENCED	

Table 5.3 Experience as a reader across the curriculum: scale 2

- My child read independently and corrected themselves when necessary.
- My child read independently without help.
- My child read independently and with expression.

Planning for learning

As class teacher, you have a professional duty to retain responsibility for the learning of each pupil in your class. In order to move towards personalising learning, though, you will want to ensure that the children have an opportunity to plan some of their own learning too.

A topic approach

One way of approaching planning for learning is to use a topic approach. Topics would need to be set for Years 1–6 across the school, ensuring that there is a range of bias. For example, some topics will have a science bias, others a historical bias and so on, so that across the year the children will have the opportunity to develop the skills needed for each discipline. Table 5.4 shows an example of a suggested topic grid for Key Stage 1.

Although topics are pre-set across the year groups, the topics themselves should be different every time they are presented because the topic should build on the children's prior knowledge and their range of interests and this will differ with every class. This can be done simply when the topic is introduced to the children.

When the topic is introduced to the class, personalise it by asking them three questions and recording their responses in the form of a mind map, which is then

SUGGESTED TOPICS FOR KEY STAGE 1						
	Autumn term		Spring term		Summer term	
YEAR 1	SEASONS AND WEATHER (geography/ science bias)	THE BODY (science and PSHE bias)	TOYS AND MACHINES (design and technology bias)	DINOSAURS (history bias)	GROWTH AND LIVING THINGS (science bias)	LOCAL ENVIRONMENT CONTRASTING WITH FARM (geography bias)
YEAR 2	JOURNEYS (geography bias)	LIGHT AND COLOUR (science bias)	MATERIALS (design and technology and science bias)	HOW PEOPLE USED TO LIVE – VICTORIAN TIMES (history and PHSE bias)	SATs	LIVING WORLD AND MINIBEASTS (science bias)

Table 5.4 A suggested topic grid for Key Stage 1

displayed in the classroom and used for review purposes across the life of the topic. The three questions are:

1 What do you already know about this topic?
2 What would you like to know? (This generates key questions.)
3 Where do you think we can find out?

By asking the children what they already know about each topic you are ascertaining their levels of understanding (or misunderstanding) and you can then build upon this prior knowledge. By asking them to generate their own agenda for the learning, you are personalising the agenda, and by asking them where they can get the information you are enabling them to think about knowledge and where it is 'seated', and you are encouraging them to learn about how they might learn best.

Figure 5.8 shows an example of a class mind map from a Year 1 class.

Some examples of where they might find out about topics have included the obvious places such as books, the library and the Internet, but other learning opportunities have been raised when someone says, 'My granddad knows about this' or 'I've been to a museum' or 'I've got a video/DVD.' Sometimes children will be an 'expert' on the topic and can be used as a resource for others in the class (including the adults) – this does wonders for a child's self-esteem.

Writing your plans

You have the class mind map that was generated during your discussion with the children. This gives you the basis of what you are going to cover. As the adult responsible for the learning in your classroom, though, you will want to ensure that the children have the opportunity to learn the necessary skills and concepts

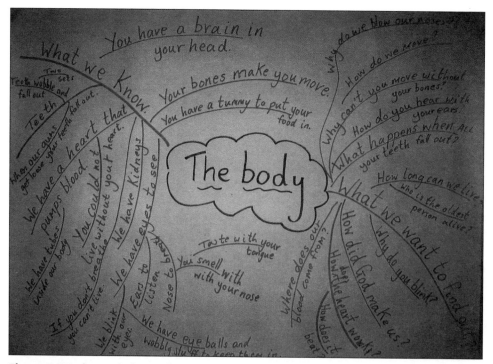

Figure 5.8 A class mind map from Year 1

related to each topic. These can be incorporated into your plan as you work on transferring the children's list to your planning documents.

On the macro level of curriculum planning you can have your topic grid and topic overview sheets (see Figures 5.9 and 5.10). These provide vital evidence of coverage of the programmes of study.

Area of Learning	Date	Date	Date	Date	Date	Date	Date	Date
Linguistic and literary								
Collaborative group reading								
Mathematical								
Scientific								
Technological								
Human and social								
Aesthetic and creative								
Physical								
Moral								
Spiritual								
MFL								

Figure 5.9 Key Stage 1 – topic overview sheet (areas of learning and experience)

Area of learning	Date	Date	Date	Date	Date	Date	Date	Date
Literacy								
Numeracy								
Science								
ICT								
History								
Geography								
Art								
D & T								
Music								
PE								
RE								
MFL								

Figure 5.10 Key Stage 1 – topic overview sheet (subjects)

On the micro level of curriculum planning you will need to decide (with your support staff) how best to record your daily and weekly plans. These planning documents should be able to respond to the changing needs of the children. You will have some possible learning objectives in mind, but, as we have discussed earlier, the children will not necessarily learn what you have planned for them to learn. Through your observations of the children at work and by your discussions with them about their developing understanding, you will see which aspects of learning need further coverage and which are secure and can be built upon.

Short-term plans should be organic documents – growing over the course of the day or week – in response to the changing learning needs of the children. I would expect to see these plans covered in annotations, sticky notes, crossings-out and scribbled additions if they are being used effectively.

It is important to mention at this point that planning sheets need to meet the needs of the teachers using them and therefore it may not be advisable to have one planning format to be used by everyone. There should be a range of planning sheets available so that staff can choose one that best meets their needs and ways of working.

Figures 5.11–14 show some examples of planning pro formas that were devised and used by my staff.

Weekly planning sheet

	Language	Maths	Science	ICT	History	Geography	Art	D & T	Music	PE	MFL
Learning objective											
Visual											
Auditory											
Kinaesthetic											

Figure 5.11

Weekly planning sheet

	Language	Maths	Science	Other areas of learning
Learning objective				
Visual				
Auditory				
Kinaesthetic				

Figure 5.12

Weekly planning sheet

	Language	Maths	Science				
Learning objective							
Visual							
Auditory							
Kinaesthetic							

Figure 5.13

Key Stage 1 planning sheet

	Language	Maths	Science	ICT	History	Geography	Art	D & T	Music	PE	MFL
Learning objective											
Linguistic											
Logical mathematical											
Musical											
Visual and spatial											
Bodily kinaesthetic											
Naturalist											
Interpersonal											
Intrapersonal											

Figure 5.14

How do you get pupils planning their own learning?

We have already spoken about whole-class brainstorming sessions whereby children contribute to the topic planning. On an individual level, some children in Year 2 will be ready to undertake a similar exercise by forming their own mind map of their key questions. They could then undertake this individual learning whenever there is a 'free time' during the learning day or week. There is never an excuse for children wasting time or opportunity to learn and having their own individualised learning plan gives them a focus for their learning.

Figures 5.15 and 5.16 depict two examples of individual mind maps made by children at the end of Year 1

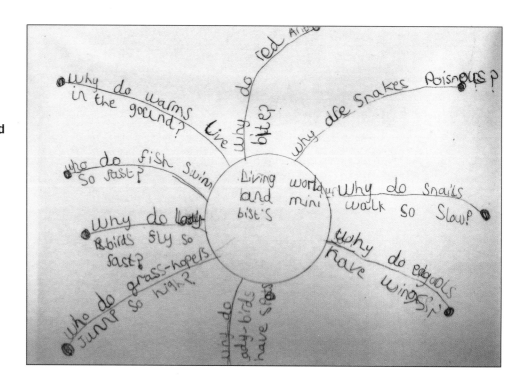

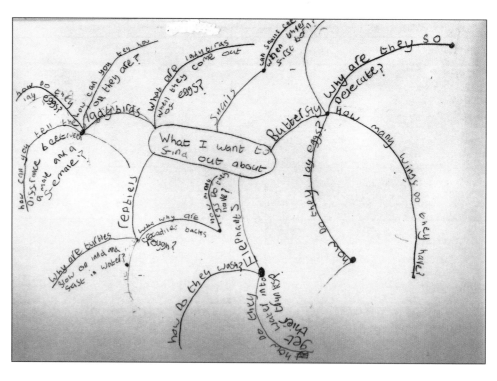

What does a typical learning day in Key Stage 1 look like?

A typical learning day in Key Stage 1 is shown as Figure 5.17.

Time	The children	The staff
9.00	• Arrive	• One member of staff is tasked to liaise with parents • Other staff welcome the children • Registration
9.20	• Attend assembly	• Attend assembly
9.30	• Group session to discuss their learning plans and the adult-led activities available	• One member of staff leads the group session • PULSE session for input
9.40	• Independently accessing and using resources to undertake a range of learning activities based on the class mind map • 'Free' time used for independent research and learning based on the child's individual mind map • Independently accessing fruit and drink • Children responsible for tidying up	• One member of staff is tasked to observe learning – either focus child/ren or focus activity • Other staff play alongside the children • PULSE sessions are 'scattered' across the learning session • Collaborative group reading session (either a.m. or p.m.) • Playtime is taken as and when appropriate
12.00	• Having lunch and joining in playtime	
1.15	• Back to class • Same pattern as morning	
3.00	• On carpet ready for group time – review of the learning day or a story or singing	• One member of staff leads the group session • Another member of staff completes the tidying up
3.15	• Getting ready to go home or to after-school club	• One member of staff stays with the group • Another member of staff is by the door to ensure that no children go home without an adult

Figure 5.17 Key Stage 1 – a typical learning day

Summary

In this chapter we have looked at personalising learning in Key Stage 1. We have considered:

- the transition between the Foundation Stage and Key Stage 1;
- getting to know your learners;
- continuing the relationship with parents;
- the learning environment;
- classroom provision and the use of resources;

- the curriculum;
- getting ready to learn;
- developing learning behaviours in children;
- provision of learning activities;
- observation of learning;
- record keeping;
- planning; and
- what a learning day may look like.

Review your current practice.

Decide how you need to **modify** it in order to implement personalising learning.

Transition to Key Stage 2

Transition to Key Stage 2 should be a much more straightforward process. The children are that much more mature and are developing positive self-images and high self-esteem and you can talk to them about their feelings about the move into Year 3.

This does not mean that you should ignore the transition, because for some children any change is painful and they need to feel confident that the process will be managed for them. This can be done as in the transition from Foundation Stage to Key Stage 1:

- with visits to their new classroom;
- with meetings with their new teacher and support staff;
- by having their new teacher visit them in their Year 2 class; and
- through story-swap sessions or class exchange for other lessons.

Transfer of information

Proper transfer of information ensures continuity and progression for the children in their learning. The learning profile that has been building up since the child entered the school should be the core of the information-transfer process. Other records, such as the developmental-reading record should also be passed into Key Stage 2.

My staff found it useful for the children's books of their recorded work to transfer with the children. This gave staff a first-hand experience of the level of work that the children had been engaged in during the previous class. This ensured that there was no opportunity for the children to 'try it on' with their new teacher, insisting that they could not work at the expected level. It also helped the children to see that learning is a continuum, it is about building on from what they can already do, developing new skills as they develop.

Some staff still found it useful to have a face-to-face meeting with the previous teacher in order to ensure that each child could be discussed in detail.

Getting to know your learners

It is important to get to know your learners so that you can continue to build on prior learning and support each pupil in their individual development as a life-long learner.

By the time the children enter Key Stage 2, most of them are at the level of maturity that ensures that they are beginning to develop a clear picture of how they learn best. With continued support throughout the Foundation Stage and Key Stage 1 they have been developing the language to describe their learning preferences and needs. So, in order to get to know your learners in Key Stage 2, ask them to tell you about what they like to learn, how they like to learn and with whom they learn best. This can be done individually and in whole-class discussions so that the pupils have a chance to hear about others' preferred ways of learning.

Observation will also still play its part in getting to know your learners. The beginning of the new school year will still be the focus for your observations of your children at their learning, but you will need to continue to observe regularly across the year to ensure that your assessments of the children remain up to date and accurate.

Continuing the relationship with parents

Although it is true that the older the child gets generally the less involved the parent becomes in their education, this does not need to be the case. Parents still have a crucial role to play in the education of their children and therefore should be kept fully informed about what is being learned and the progress that their child is making. They should also be engaged in discussions about future learning plans to continue to ensure that learning is facilitated beyond the school gates.

Meeting the parents formally

As in Key Stage 1 classes, it is important that you meet with the parents as early as possible in the new school year, so that you can discuss their child's progress. At this stage, it is useful for the child to be invited to be a part of the discussion, too. Expectations can be discussed and this could also be the time that targets could be agreed between all parties.

Meeting the parents informally

This can be more difficult as the children move through Key Stage 2, as they are wanting to assert their independence and are not keen for their parents to be coming into the playground to drop them off or collect them from school.

I would suggest that it is still good practice for a member of staff to collect the children from the playground at the start of the school day and accompany them to the playground at the end, thereby affording an opportunity to meet informally with those parents who are there. This maintains contact with the parents and can prevent minor issues becoming great big problems that they have to come in and see you about.

If you need to make contact with a parent who is not available at the beginnings and ends of the school day, then a more formal approach by making an appointment will have to suffice. Hopefully, you have developed close relationships with the parents and can do this without its seeming like a 'big deal'. Otherwise, a phone call may be all that is needed.

Keeping parents informed

As in Key Stage 1, the weekly planning sheet should be displayed so that the parents have ready access to this information. For those parents who are not able to bring or collect their children to and from school, the topic information sheet (as used in Key Stage 1) can be completed and sent home at the start of every new topic. Why not get the children to write it – providing a real purpose for writing?

The topic information sheet can continue to be supplemented with termly meetings between the teachers and the parents from each year group. This enables parents to ask questions of clarification and gives staff an opportunity to explain the planned learning for the coming term.

The children can also play a role in keeping their parents informed about their learning. This can be done in several ways. Records of learning can travel between home and school via:

- the self-assessment booklet (PEPI);
- the homework diary;
- the reading diary; and
- individual learning plans, target sheets and mind maps.

Regular sessions can be arranged whereby pupils invite their parents to visit the classroom. The child can then show their work – in their books and in displays – and talk to their parents about their next steps in learning.

The important thing is that the child sees that home and school are still working closely together in order to support their learning.

Learning environment

The safe emotional climate needs to be maintained in Key Stage 2 classes. By this stage, the children should have developed a positive self-image and should be aware of their strengths and areas for further development. They should be encouraged to continue to take learning risks so the adults will need to be responsible for maintaining the right balance of challenge and support.

Although the children are maturing and should be more able to manage their emotions effectively, some children can still be extremely vulnerable in Key Stage 2, particularly in Years 5 and 6, as their hormones begin to impact on their idea of self.

The Golden Rules will continue to apply but the children can take on more responsibility for monitoring their own and each other's behaviour. Issues arising can be discussed in circle time.

Circle time discussions can be used to great effect in Key Stage 2, with the children taking on more responsibility for choosing the topics for discussion. The relationships in the class will be well developed by this stage (particularly if the class has been together since the Foundation Stage) and so the children will be able to discuss potentially difficult topics, most of which will be based on their real-life experiences.

Adults leading these sessions will need to be particularly sensitive to individual responses during the discussions in order to highlight any pupils who may need further individual support in bubble time.

An important aspect of the learning environment remains the establishment of a supportive emotional climate. You are expecting the children to be independent in their learning, as far as possible, but there will be times when they will become 'stuck' in their learning. Children need to know what to do when they don't know what to do. You need to discuss with them that it is perfectly normal to get 'stuck' sometimes and get the children discussing the strategies they use when this happens. Get the children to make a learning poster about how to get 'unstuck' and display it in the classroom – the poster should be added to as more strategies are discovered.

The poster would include the following:

- stop and think for a while;
- take a break for some fresh air or water;
- get support or advice from your friends;
- use resources for learning, such as dictionaries, thesauruses, word lists;
- use reference books;
- use the Internet;
- use a calculator; and
- ask an adult (this should be a last resort).

Children need to be encouraged to solve their own problems wherever possible in order to develop their independence and gain confidence from being independent. Asking people to solve their own problems empowers them and often contributes to increased self-esteem. If we always solve problems for people, we make them dependent and devalue them. So, if anyone comes with a problem, remember that your initial response is, 'And what are you going to do about it?'.

CHECKLIST

Use the checklist questions from the Foundation Stage and Key Stage 1 and add:

- Are the adults in Key Stage 2 sensitive to the changing emotional needs of the children?

> - Are the children taking the lead in organising their own learning environment?
> - Are the children encouraged to be self-regulating of their own behaviour and of that of others around them?
> - Are the children expected to be as independent as they feel comfortable with, in managing their relationships as well as their learning?
>
> Review your learning environment.
> What changes do you need to introduce so that your learning environment facilitates personalising learning?

Classroom routines

Encourage the children to become involved in managing the routines in their classroom. Get them to devise time-saving ways of undertaking everyday tasks in order to maximise time for learning. Encourage them to take on responsibility for ensuring that their learning environment is always well resourced, tidy and well organised.

Continue with the established routines from Key Stage 1:

- lining-up routines;
- changing for PE; and
- flexible playtimes.

Classroom provision and use of resources

By the time children reach Key Stage 2, they should be familiar with school equipment and resources and should have been taught how to use them safely and effectively.

The learning resources available will contribute to setting the right kind of climate for personalising learning, and, if we want our children to develop as independent learners, we should not be doing things for them that they are more than capable of doing for themselves. By taking this approach you are also reducing some of the administrative burden traditionally shouldered by the staff.

Adult–pupil ratio

I would always recommend that there be at least two adults to every classroom, even in Key Stage 2. This enables the effective use of groups for learning; it provides individual support for those who need it; and it enables the adults to have the time to focus on their observational assessments of learning that will in turn impact on future planning.

Materials and resources

A range of resources will need to be provided. This includes:

- resources for self-help;
- resources for research; and
- resources for making and doing.

The children should be shouldering the responsibility of organising resources for themselves within their learning environment, ensuring that the resources they need are ready and available for use and cleaned and stored once finished with.

The children could be responsible for ensuring that at least once a term:

- the learning equipment is 'spring-cleaned';
- a list is generated of things that need replacing; and
- a list of new equipment and resources that they would like to have in their classroom is generated.

Display

Children in Key Stage 2 classes should almost be assuming full responsibility for the displays within their classroom. They should be able to design and plan the displays, mount their own work, make the captions and banners to accompany the displays and so on. The only aspect of display that they will probably need assistance with is the actual mounting of the display on the wall, because of the safety issues involved in working at heights.

Grouping children for learning

In order to maximise learning opportunities, most of my staff opted to work with mixed-ability groups. They found that it provided a means of ensuring equal opportunities, encouraged social integration and cooperative behaviour, provided positive role models for the less able pupils and forced staff to acknowledge that the pupils in their class were thought of in terms of their individuality. Groups were not fixed and they would be formed depending on task requirements.

When I talk about group work, I mean genuine group work, not just collections of pupils for administrative purposes or for the convenience of sharing limited resources. Genuine group work takes place when children actively collaborate with each other to achieve a finished product. It encourages collaboration and cooperation and creates genuine learning opportunities as they learn from each other. The group monitor and direct themselves and become less reliant on adults. This encourages task talk rather than social talk, and it has been shown to keep children focused on their task for longer periods.

If you are going to use group work successfully, you need to ensure that certain conditions are in place. The children need to:

- be seated so that they can work together;
- be given time to complete tasks;
- be taught appropriate group-working skills;
- be given roles initially, though eventually they will be responsible for the assignment of roles, e.g. timekeeper, scribe;

- be given explanations about helping one another;
- be given much public group praise or minimal private group reprimand; and
- be given real collaborative tasks.

So what real group tasks can we give them? You can use groups to:

- consider what has been said (do they agree/disagree, have they any questions?);
- get ideas (brainstorm or mind-map activities);
- expand on ideas (pass brainstorms or mind-maps between groups so that new ideas can be added);
- work on a single task (e.g. learning posters, writing stories, devising a quiz, dramatic role play or dance);
- debate issues (divide the group into pro and con and give them time to prepare their arguments); and
- devise questions for a visitor or a hot-seat activity.

There are many tasks that can be assigned to a group.

If children are going to work together in groups, they will need to develop their understanding of group roles and the skills needed to be an effective team player. These roles and skills will need to be introduced and discussed and, as with the introduction of anything new, the first few attempts will probably be disastrous. But, if you keep persevering with group work and provide feedback to the groups on not only the 'product' of their labours but also the process skills that they used, they will develop their effectiveness at group working.

They need to know that it is a useful thing to do to establish ground rules for group working before they begin. Perhaps this could be done as a whole-class activity, displayed as a learning poster and added to as new ideas arise. On this learning poster you would hope to see such things as taking it in turns to speak (maybe even numbering speakers to begin with so that everyone gets a turn). They should include active listening as a key skill – really listening to what the person before you has said and building on it, not going off on your own tangent. You would hope that they would include such things as accepting that everyone is entitled to their point of view but that it can be further explored, questioned and mediated by listening to the opinions of others. You would hope that they would learn to compromise sometimes and understand that their idea cannot always be the one chosen. By observing the groups at work, you can offer feedback on their performance against the objectives they have set themselves on their learning poster, supporting the development of these skills.

As they become more advanced in their group-working skills, they will be able to provide feedback to each other on their individual performance within the group and will be able to evaluate how successful they were in their group working. They can then record their skill-development progress on their PEPI record and consider what they need to work on next.

Geoff Hannan (2001) has undertaken a lot of research into effective group working, particularly paired work, with emphasis on the effect of gender in grouping. He argues that if you pair boys together because of the way their brains work, one boy will take the lead and the other will follow, and there will be little language interaction between them. If you pair a boy with a girl, more communication will take place. The boy will need to be more reflective in his communication and the girl will need to be more speculative. Both boys and girls will be enhancing and developing their core language and learning skills and the boy will also be extending his social skills.

Hannan says that, when planning your paired and group work, you should plan for one-third to be in friendship pairings or groupings; one-third to be in single-gender, non-friendship pairings and groupings; and one-third to be in mixed-gender pairings and groupings. This should take the form of a rolling programme so that, during the time span of half a term, each pupil will have worked in a structured way with every other pupil in the class. In our school we called this system of pairing *study buddies* or *learning partners*.

If you build into this programme of study buddies or learning partners, as a matter of course, a feedback system so that children are receiving feedback on their performance as a learning partner from a range of learning partners they have worked with, each child will be building a very detailed picture of themselves as a learner within that context.

CHECKLIST

Use the checklists from the Foundation Stage and Key Stage 1 and add:

- Are children encouraged to be totally independent as learners in your classroom?
- Are the children encouraged to make their own resources for learning support, e.g. learning posters?
- Are the children responsible for the maintenance of an effective learning environment?
- Are you using groups effectively within your classroom?

Review your classroom provision.
What changes do you need to introduce so that your classroom provision facilitates personalising learning?

Curriculum

You have already considered what kind of curriculum you want to be working towards in Key Stage 1. This approach to the curriculum should be extended and built upon in Key Stage 2.

Extending your existing curriculum and building upon it will ensure continuity and progression in learning for your pupils.

Building on the Key Stage 1 curriculum

You have decided whether your approach to the curriculum is going to be a subject-based, discipline-based or cross-curricular topic approach. You will have an agreed curriculum model showing how your curriculum serves a personalising learning agenda. Hopefully, you will have PSHE, including citizenship and learning skills, as the core of your curriculum. Table 6.1 shows an example of a core curriculum for Key Stage 2.

SKILLS	KNOWLEDGE AND UNDERSTANDING
Independence and responsibility Assertiveness Self-esteem Feelings	• Set own goals, both academically and socially • Manage a variety of social situations • Empathise with the feelings of others • Present oneself positively to others • Take responsibility for own actions and outcomes arising from these
Respect for people, environment and property	• Be aware of and respect individual differences • Continue to develop an understanding of different cultures/religions • Use resources effectively and economically • Demonstrate an awareness of their locality • Continue to develop the ability to speak other languages
Healthy lifestyle	• Be responsible/independent for own personal hygiene/safety in and out of school • Demonstrate awareness of and maintain healthy eating and exercise in order to keep healthy • Be given opportunities to experience a variety of physical exercise and be encouraged to participate by choice in extra-curricular activities
Play an active role in society	• Care for one another • Value and take an active role in school life and the wider community
Managing relationships in a variety of contexts	• Demonstrate respect for others feelings, decisions, rights, etc. • Demonstrate the ability to use the language of mediation • Understand and demonstrate the skills required for effective group working
Effective communicator	• Understand the value of and demonstrate the ability to communicate in a variety of forms • Value and evaluate different points of view • Be confident to offer own views and ideas • Demonstrate the ability to negotiate effectively
Problem solving	• Be aware that problems have more than one solution • Demonstrate the ability to plan, implement and evaluate a solution • Demonstrate the ability to problem-solve within a group
Research skills	• Understand and demonstrate how to research effectively • Demonstrate the ability to use the library for research • Demonstrate the ability to use the Internet for research • Understand the difference between fact, bias and opinion
Thinking skills	• Understand their learning preferences • Demonstrate the ability to construct a logical argument

Table 6.1 An example of a core curriculum for Key Stage 2

Getting ready to learn

As discussed earlier, we know that the brain can be switched off learning by anxiety and when basic needs are not met. It therefore becomes essential to think about ways of 'grounding' our children to prepare them mentally and physically for learning.

Meditation

Instead of yoga, use meditation sessions at the beginning of the afternoon (following a hectic lunchtime period) or if the children are particularly boisterous after a playtime. An adult uses music to create a positive, relaxed atmosphere and takes the children and other adults through the meditation exercises.

The children should sit cross-legged either on their own or with a partner (back to back). They should be encouraged to think about their posture and sit with a good straight back. They should find a focus point for their eyes or close their eyes and concentrate on their breathing. They should be taught to breathe in through their noses to a count of five and blow out slowly through their mouths to a count of ten for a few breaths until they feel calm and relaxed. They should then sit still, calm, quiet and focused for up to fifteen minutes. The adult (or child) leading the session should then bring them slowly out of their meditation, by leading some stretching and deep-breathing exercises.

The leader might say, 'Reach out your arms in front of you, cross your hands at the wrist and turn your palms together so that you can hold your hands. While still holding your hands together, raise them up slowly until they are above your head, arms level or behind your ears. Hold this pose while you breathe deeply in and out [as described above] twice. Slowly lower the arms. Relax.'

Brain Gym®

The children have been introduced to Brain Gym® in Key Stage 1 and understand that the use of the exercises can re-energise them and help refocus them to improve their learning. You can introduce new exercises to the children or extend ones that they already know as a class activity, but then the children should begin to recognise in themselves the need to be re-energised and could use the exercises for themselves or within their working groups if they see that they are becoming stale and less productive.

You can use all the Brain Gym® exercises shown in Chapter 5 but you can build on them, develop them and introduce more difficult moves in Key Stage 2 – the children love the challenge. Here are some ways to increase the challenge of the exercises.

Cross-lateral working

To build on Key Stage 1 cross-lateral working exercises:

● reach behind the body to touch the opposite foot, then alternate; and
● skip between each cross-crawl.

To improve balance, do cross-crawl exercises with your eyes closed. A more complicated exercise is this one:

- With your thumb and first finger, to grasp the opposite ear lobe. With your other thumb and first finger, pinch your nose gently. Try swapping as quickly as you can.

Lazy 8s

- When you feel ready, draw your lazy 8s with the arm that is not the one you use for writing.
- Try drawing your lazy 8s with both arms together.

Time to loosen up

Children are always sitting down at school and can become tense. This exercise helps to relax the body, loosening up muscles that have become cramped from sitting too long. It should help to re-energise.

- Stand, cross your legs and relax your knees slightly. Let your head, the upper part of your body and your arms hang forward. Try to keep relaxed. Swing gently from left to right, like a giant pendulum. Swing three or four times. Then come up slowly, cross your legs the other way and repeat the exercise.

Double doodles

Drawing with both hands at once activates hand–eye coordination.

- Use a finger to draw a doodle in the air.
- Let your other hand join in and try to mirror your other hand.
- Doodle fast, doodle slowly.
- Try writing your name in the air.
- With your other hand, write your name backwards.
- Try to write with both hands at the same time – forwards with one hand and backwards with the other.

Alphabet aerobics

- Saying the alphabet, raise the left arm into the air if the capital letter has only straight lines, the right arm if it has only curved lines and both arms if it is formed with both straight and curved lines.
- Try saying the alphabet backwards while doing the aerobic exercises.

Developing learning behaviours in children

Continue to introduce the learning objective at the beginning of every session and get the children to discuss what it means and what the success criteria for that activity should be – they will be well practised at this by now.

Use the traffic-light fans that the children made in Key Stage 1 during group times, until they let you know that they are too mature to do so. This will probably be towards the end of Year 3. At that time, discuss with them other ways of showing you that they have understood the task and other ways of engaging in self-assessment.

They should be well experienced in providing focused, constructive feedback to each other now on their strengths as a learning partner or group worker, so you can get them to think about giving feedback in terms of what other people need to work on in order to improve. This will need to be modelled for the children so that they know to offer criticism in a positive and supportive way in order to help other people to grow and develop.

This will help them to be assertive in their relationships in and beyond the school, into adulthood. This is another vital lifelong skill.

Building in choice for children

See the section of this title in Chapter 5 (page 82), where we discuss Key Stage 1. If you have implemented some of the suggestions included in that section, by now your children will be used to being responsible for organising a large proportion of their learning week.

Your role in Key Stage 2 classes is to ensure that the children maintain the momentum of managing their own learning time and make the best use of the time to ensure that they are developing their learning skills.

Learning activities

You will need to maintain a balance between adult-led learning activities, to ensure that they are receiving the necessary input to facilitate continued skill development, and pupil-led activities, providing them with opportunities to display their learning in whatever way they feel appropriate. You will, of course, be closely monitoring every child's work to ensure that they are developing skills in presenting their learning in a variety of ways and not always in the same form.

Developing the five Rs

1 Resilience

By this stage in the children's learning career, they should have a range of strategies to support them when they get 'stuck'. They should have contributed to learning posters displayed on their classroom walls, which have a list of things to do when they don't know what to do. The last resort for them at this stage should be to ask a grown up.

2 Resourcefulness

The children will be well aware as to the resources and facilities that your school can provide for them and should know where to access the resources that they need and how to use them effectively.

3 Reflectiveness

The children will understand fully by now the importance of taking time to reflect on the outcomes of their learning activities. They will have developed a wide vocabulary to describe their reflections on their own learning and on the learning of others.

They should be encouraged to become involved in marking their own work before handing it in to the teacher for marking. They should be able to highlight for themselves:

- places in their work where they have clearly met the success criteria; and
- places in their work where they think they could make improvements, including checking of spellings, grammar and punctuation.

They can be encouraged to work with their study buddy or learning partner on marking each other's work, using the three-to-one rule – three places in the work where they clearly met the success criteria and one place where further improvement could be made.

4 Remembering

Continue to use learning posters that the children have made in support of their learning for the topics that they are studying. The children will know by now how to use these posters effectively.

You will find that an interesting conversation to have with the children is about their 'remembering place'. Ask the children to consider where they remember things, whether they see things written or drawn in their remembering place, whether they are in uppercase or lowercase, in colour or black and white – encourage the children actively to place things in their remembering place in their head. This creative visualisation technique will assist greatly in retaining information.

5 Responsiveness

By this stage, the children should be managing their emotions and feelings with confidence. You will still need to make time for discussions about how they feel about new experiences and how they manage themselves in new situations, to ensure that you work with the changing worlds that the children find themselves in as their social circle expands and they become more independent of their parents.

Reading resources

You will be maintaining your approach to providing as wide a range of reading resources as possible. The children could be asked if they have particular preferences for reading material, e.g. a favourite genre, a favourite author, a favourite subject, that could then be made available to them.

The children can be responsible for keeping a record of the books they have read. This can be combined with a critical review of the book that could then be displayed to aid other children in making appropriate choices of what to read.

Groups for reading

Maintain the use of mixed-ability collaborative groups for reading.

Later in the chapter, when we look at record keeping, we will see a suggested format that can be used for recording skill development of your collaborative reading groups.

Listening to children read

You are still focusing on skill development as you are listening to the children read in Key Stage 2 and hopefully you will be encouraging the children to reflect for themselves on their developing skills. Get them talking in their groups to each other about the strategies that they use for making sense in their reading, so that they can continue to learn from each other. Encourage them to be determining for themselves what they think they should work on next in their reading.

Writing

You will continue to offer a wide variety of writing-for-real-purpose experiences for the children and support them in their writing with a range of planning frameworks, ideas boxes and vocabulary lists and so forth. The difference is that, in Key Stage 2, the children should be encouraged to devise and add to these support materials for themselves, because they will know what works for them.

As the pupils mature as writers, the planning formats will become more sophisticated, with children learning that more things than one happen in a story, so the planning sheets will need to reflect this and provide space for the 'and thens'.

At this stage, the children should be expected to produce quality writing. This can be done only by spending time on planning, editing, revising and redrafting the work over a period of time. This should mean the children will be expected to produce fewer pieces of completed written work, while being provided with many more opportunities to work on sections of written material, e.g. beginnings, characterisations, settings, endings.

Using the agreed marking strategies, every child will receive the same amount of feedback regardless of their ability, i.e. three places where they have met the learning objective and one where they could make some improvement. This type of focused marking can take some time, particularly as the children progress through Key Stage 2 and write more and more.

The children can continue to be involved in marking the work of their study buddy and provide formative feedback to encourage further improvement. These aspects for improvement can be discussed during plenary sessions, so that all the children have the opportunity to hear about what makes a good piece of writing even better.

ICT

By now the children will have a wide range of skills and understandings about the use of ICT in their learning. They can use ICT for the presentation and storage of their work – they should all have their own work folder and their own email address and should be using the Internet for research as a matter of course.

Key Stage 2 SATs

You should adopt the same approach to Key Stage 2 SATs that you adopted in Key Stage 1 – they should not be allowed to skew the curriculum and learning experience of the children.

If you want to engage in some revision activities with the children, you could get them to:

- set each other questions or quizzes;
- talk through their methods of approaching difficult questions;
- construct mind maps and pole-bridge them with their learning partner (this is where you use your finger to trace your lines of thought and talk aloud at the same time about the knowledge encapsulated in the mind map – this helps firmly seal the learning in the memory and children should be able to visualise their mind map even when it is no longer in front of them);
- make learning posters for revision purposes;
- be honest about what they find most difficult in their learning and pair them with someone who can offer suggestions on how to approach it more positively;
- make up mnemonics and share them with others; and
- talk about all of the strategies that they have developed in their school career that have helped them to become effective learners.

Most of all, make sure that the children stay calm, relaxed and focused – citrus oil in aromatherapy burners may help. Ensure that they have plenty of fresh air and water to aid concentration and keep their confidence levels high. Reassure them that they are going to do well because you know that they are all experienced learners who know how to approach new learning with confidence. Remind them to read the questions thoroughly before answering; make sure that they provide supporting evidence for their answers to show their thinking and check their answers before handing in their papers to ensure that they have not made any silly mistakes.

Observation of learning

As an adult supporting and assessing learning development in the children, you will need to continue to observe and record your observations of the children's development as learners, but by now the children should also be developing skills in self-monitoring and self-evaluation. Being self-aware as a learner is a key skill for lifelong learning.

Self-assessment

The children have been working with their PEPI assessment programme since Key Stage 1 and are used to the system of either choosing a key skill to work on from their 'I can' statements or having someone point out to them that they have achieved success in a key skill area. They know that they have to provide evidence of their achievement, which could be an advocate to speak on their behalf as well as pieces of work.

The 'I can' statements for Key Stage 2 are obviously going to be more sophisticated and therefore will probably take a longer time to achieve, but when they were written we tried to build in progression or split a target into smaller, more achievable parts to ensure that the children could see that they were continuing to make good progress in the development of their key skills.

We decided to put our Key Stage 2 targets in the form of an A5 booklet that the children would keep with them throughout the whole Key Stage. A summary sheet was then provided as a last page to the booklet, to aid the child in summarising their learning and development in the key skills.

Presentation skills:

- I am proud of my appearance and always try to be smart and well presented.
- I can mount my own work.
- I can keep my files/folders/drawer in good order.
- I can write neatly in joined-up handwriting.
- I always check my work for accuracy before handing it in.
- My writing is interesting for others to read.
- I know how to present work for different contexts, e.g. maths, science, story.
- I speak clearly in a variety of contexts.

Time-management skills:

- I plan ahead so that I can use time well.
- I can organise my time to maximise learning.
- My homework is always completed on time.
- My work in class is always completed on time.
- I can set myself realistic time targets for work.

Research skills:

- I can use a variety of sources for my research, e.g. books, encyclopaedias, libraries, museums, magazines and newspapers, television and my community.
- I can use the Internet for research.
- I can use the Dewey system in the library to access the books I want.
- I can sort the information from my research and present it in my own words.

Communication skills:

- I can speak to a large audience and be heard.
- I can speak to different groups of people in an appropriate, accurate and concise manner.
- I can write in an appropriate manner to different groups of people.
- I can empathise with others.
- I understand that body language is an important part of communication and can use it effectively.
- I can listen actively.
- I can read, recognise and understand important or relevant written information.
- I can use ICT as a means of communication.

Organisation skills:

- I can organise my working space.
- I can keep my working environment tidy and well organised.
- I can organise myself in order to achieve my objectives.
- I can recognise desired outcomes and work to achieve them constructively.

Team working – interpersonal skills:

- I can work harmoniously and constructively with others in a joint activity.
- I can respect and tolerate the values and beliefs of others within a joint activity.
- I can communicate effectively, as a member of a team, in order to convince others of my point of view.
- I can give feedback to people in my group on their performance.
- I can accept constructive criticism from others in my group to enable me to improve my performance.
- I can share the same working environment and respect the differing needs of others.
- I can work in lots of different teams.

Problem-solving and decision-making skills:

- I understand that many problems have more than one solution.
- I can recognise and identify a problem.
- I can gather information and data to help me think about a problem.
- I can consider a variety of approaches to a problem.
- I understand that if I make a decision I have to live with the consequences.
- I understand that decisions I make impact on others.
- I know how to listen to the opinions of others when making joint decisions.
- I understand that sometimes other people will make decisions that impact on me.

Figure 6.1 PEPI statements for Key Stage 2

In the Key Stage 2 PEPI booklet, each key skill was put onto a separate page, which allowed the children to identify other areas of potential skill development in each area. The last page was boxed and headed 'My personal assessment', with a space for the child's signature and the date. Towards the end of Year 6, the children would be asked to undertake a review before completing this assessment page. They would then be asked to record a summary assessment of their strengths and areas that they feel could do with further development. They could then use this information to help them complete the transfer sheet for their secondary school (Chapter 7).

The adults' role in this system of self-evaluation was to remind the children of PEPI through such opportunities as circle time and assembly. During whole-class sessions the adults would ensure that the process of learning was discussed, including the development of learning skills, rather than just revising the learning outcomes in terms of products.

Adults observing learning

You will be continuing your observations and feedback to the children and parents on what you observe, ensuring that they too have the opportunity to input from their perspectives on their observations.

You will probably not be making formal written observations of the children at their learning, in the same way as happened in the Foundation Stage and Key Stage 1, but rather just be more generally aware of the learning skills in each pupil as they develop. You will need to make notes of significant leaps in the learning so that this information can be added to the learning profile – this could be done using sticky notes.

Record keeping

As we have seen already, you need to keep records to ensure that you maintain an accurate and up-to-date record of each child as a developing learner. The children can take on more responsibility for the upkeep of their day-to-day records, such as records of what they have been reading, scores in mental maths quizzes, scores in spelling quizzes.

Maintaining the learning profile

You should continue to maintain each child's individual learning profile at least twice a term. This will ensure that no children slip through the net. As the children mature, you could start to share this learning profile with them and see if they would want to change anything or add anything from their own observations of themselves as developing lifelong learners.

Work sampling

The children should be playing an increasing role in keeping their portfolio up to date. It can be built into their half-termly work plan that they are responsible for choosing at least two samples of their work to go into their portfolio. They can also take over responsibility for ensuring the completion of the annotation sheet that accompanies their work – this should include their own comments as well as the comments of an adult.

Reading records

Reading records from Key Stage 1 should have been passed on into Key Stage 2 and continue to be used for recording reading skill development. The reading records should be discussed with the children so that they become aware of the next steps in their reading-skill development.

You may want to keep a record of the reading-skill development of your collaborative reading groups. Figure 6.2 shows an example of a record sheet for that purpose. You would need five sheets – one for each reading group (the children should be allowed to choose the name of their reading group). On each sheet you would record the names of the children in that group, and across the top the name of the book being read and the learning objectives for each session. You can then record, in each child's row, their progress against that learning objective.

Planning for learning

Planning for possible learning outcomes remains your professional responsibility.

A topic approach

You can continue to use the topic approach established in Key Stage 1, using the same three questions with the children:

1 What do you already know about this topic?
2 What would you like to know?
3 Where might we find out?

Group:				Term:				
	Week Beg.	Week Beg.	Week Beg.	Week Beg.	Week Beg.	Week Beg.	Week Beg.	Week Beg.
Names	Focus	Focus	Focus	Focus	Focus	Focus	Focus	Focus

Figure 6.2 A typical reading record

At this stage, the children could be responsible for constructing the class mind map and could use it regularly for review purposes. They will understand by now that learning is an organic process; that by studying one question and looking for answers they may well end up with further questions. The class mind map should be used as an organic document – being added to, annotated, scribbled on – as the learning journey progresses.

Table 6.2 shows a suggested topic grid for Key Stage 2.

If your Key Stage 2 pupils continue the practice of devising their own individual topic mind maps as well as the class one, to offer a further flexible pathway, they can have some time during the learning week to work on these. They can also work on their individualised learning when they have completed all teacher-directed tasks too, so you need never worry about finding filler activities again. We found that some children would become so engaged in their individualised learning that it would spill over into their out-of-hours learning and be taken home as homework – thus releasing the teacher from setting homework activities.

Flexible pathways can be built into your planning. If you have teachers or support staff who have a specialism, then you could set up, as a minimum, one session a week or a half-term whereby the staff offer a particular subject or aspect of learning and the children can choose where they go and what interests they pursue. This needs to be well organised, otherwise it can be chaotic, but it is a

KEY STAGE 2 TOPIC GRID

	Autumn term		Spring term		Summer term	
YEAR 3	PLANETS AND SPACE (science bias)	WATER (science bias)	ROMANS (history bias)	PLANTS (science bias)	LOCAL ENVIRONMENT CONTRASTING AREA (geography bias)	FORCES (science bias)
YEAR 4	LIGHT AND SOUND (science bias)	ELECTRICITY (science bias)	TUDORS (history bias)	FOOD AND FARMING (ST LUCIA) (geography bias)	LOCAL STUDY HISTORY AND GEOGRAPHY (geography bias)	MATERIALS (science bias)
YEAR 5	ANCIENT GREECE (history bias)	FORCES (science bias)	BRITAIN SINCE 1930 (history bias)	LIVING THINGS ANIMALS AND PLANTS (science bias)	RIVERS (geography bias)	CONTRASTING UK (WALTON ON THE NAZE) (geography bias)
YEAR 6	ANCIENT EGYPT (history bias)	HUMAN BODY (science bias)	MATERIALS (science bias)		SATS	TOPOGRAPHY (geography bias)

Table 6.2 A suggested topic grid for Key Stage 2

very worthwhile activity, as children are learning from someone who has a passion or expertise in that area. Apprentice learning, in this way, can be a very powerful experience.

For example, one of our teachers set up a 'thinking group' in which children could discuss philosophical questions. This was found to be so successful that our Years 3 and 4 teachers set up thinking groups within their classes and provided questions for children to discuss in mixed-ability groups as part of their daily activities. The questions were sometimes maths problems, word quizzes or issues for debate. The children were expected to discuss solutions and/or ideas, thinking as much about the processes they were working through as the 'answer'. Creative solutions were then discussed during a plenary session. This helped the children develop their understanding about thinking – in that there was no right way to think, just a range of ways of thinking about issues or problems. Discussing the process in this way provided opportunities for the children to learn from each other.

Writing your plans

Towards the end of Key Stage 2 the children should also be enabled to have input into the weekly plans produced by the adults. A planning session can be incorporated into the end of the previous week during a group time. The children could be encouraged to provide suggestions for possible learning activities that would meet the learning objectives.

They should also be engaging in evaluation of their learning too, saying what worked for them and what didn't. This will provide vital feedback to the adults, helping them with future planning, ensuring that they incorporate more of the strategies that were deemed by the children to be successful in facilitating learning.

I would suggest that, for the purpose of accountability, you continue to complete a topic-overview sheet to ensure that you are providing coverage of the National Curriculum programmes of study. You could use the same format suggested in Chapter 5, which dealt with Key Stage 1.

As in Key Stage 1, the layout of the weekly and/or daily plans needs to meet the needs of the people using them, so no one format should be enforced. You can continue to use formats that were successful in Key Stage 1 or get the staff to devise their own.

We looked at several ways of facilitating this planning process, trying to save time for teachers to spend on being creative in their preparation of activities rather than spending endless hours writing about it in their plans. We considered resources that would support this process. One of the best we found, which was eventually purchased for all staff to use, was Curriculum Complete, a computerised planning system produced by the Skills Factory (www.skillsfactory.com).

Some of my staff also liked to record their planning for their collaborative group reading (CGR) on a separate sheet that could then be displayed in the classroom so that the children could be self-organising. A suggested pro forma for that planning is set out in Table 6.3.

	Monday	Tuesday	Wednesday	Thursday	Friday
Class:				Week beginning:	
Group Book title	CGR				
Group Book title		CGR			
Group Book title			CGR		
Group Book title				CGR	
Group Book title					CGR

Figure 6.3 A weekly planning sheet for collaborative group reading

How do you get pupils planning their own learning?

The children can be expected to plan for their own learning from Year 3. Our children devised a planning or target sheet (see Figures 6.4 and 6.5), whereby they would pick a target for themselves, which could be in any area of their learning, and they would use any 'free' time that they had during the learning week to work on their target. There would also be sessions during the week when target work would be an option. This would usually be during collaborative group reading time.

At the end of the learning week the child would review the outcomes of their learning and evaluate their level of success in meeting their target in a meeting with an adult. The child would be expected to produce evidence of their learning or an advocate who could validate their learning if it was not a 2D or 3D piece of work. The target sheet would then be signed off by the adult and the child would choose their next target to work on.

While the children were encouraged to make their own choice for their target each week, some children may need guidance or support in choosing an appropriate target.

Name:	Class:
Date:	
Target:	
I achieved this target by:	
What I will do next is …	
How I felt about my learning: ☺ ☺ ☹	

Figure 6.4 Target sheet for Years 3 and 4

My chosen target	
Planning and research	
Resources	
Evaluation	
Date: My signature:	

Figure 6.5 Target sheet for Years 5 and 6

What does a typical day in Key Stage 2 look like?

Table 6.3 illustrates what a typical Key Stage 2 day might look like.

Time	The children	The staff
9.00	• Arrive	• One member of staff is tasked to liaise with the parents • Other staff welcome the children • Registration
9.20	• Attend assembly	• Attend assembly
9.30	• Group session to discuss their learning plans and the adult-led activities available	• One member of staff leads the group session • PULSE session for input
9.40	• Independently accessing and using resources to undertake a range of learning activities based on the class mind-map • 'Free' time used for independent research and learning based on the child's individual mind map • Independently accessing fruit and drink • Children responsible for tidying up	• One member of staff is tasked to support learning for focus group or child/ren • Other staff provide support to other learners, as requested • PULSE sessions are 'scattered' across the learning session • Collaborative group reading session (either a.m. or p.m.) • Playtime is taken as and when appropriate
12.00	• Having lunch and joining in playtime	
1.00	• Back to class • Meditation followed by thinking groups	
1.40	• Same pattern as morning	
3.00	• On carpet ready for group time – review of the learning day • Story or singing	• All staff to be part of the group session for learning review
3.15	• Getting ready to go home or to after-school club	• One member of staff takes the class to the playground to meet parents

Table 6.3 Key Stage 2 – a typical day

Summary

In this chapter we have looked at personalising learning in Key Stage 2. We have considered:

● the transition between Key Stages 1 and 2;
● getting to know your learners;
● continuing the relationship with parents;
● the learning environment;
● classroom provision and the use of resources;
● the curriculum;

- getting ready to learn;
- developing learning behaviours in children;
- provision of learning activities;
- observation of learning;
- record keeping;
- planning; and
- what a learning day may look like.

Review your current practice.

Decide how you need to modify it in order to implement personalising learning.

CHAPTER 7

Transfer to Secondary School

There are two aspects of transition that you will want to consider:

- preparing your pupils for secondary school; and
- preparing the secondary schools for your pupils.

If you consistently implement policies and practices to introduce personalising learning in your school, by the end of Year 6 your children will have very clear pictures of themselves as learners – that they can evidence with the use of their PEPI record book. They are used to being treated as independent learners, playing a large part in determining what they will learn and how they will learn it. The learning environment in their secondary schools may be very different. It would not be fair to the children or the secondary schools if they were to transfer without adequate preparation.

Preparing the pupils for transfer

It is important that you have discussions with the children about their concerns and worries about secondary school. If possible, get the head of Year 7 to come along and listen to some of these concerns or an ex-Year 6 pupil who can give honest first-hand accounts of their experiences on transfer.

The children will have experienced working with a variety of adults while in the relative safety of their primary school, but the switch in secondary to changing teachers every lesson is a daunting prospect for most of them. There are bound to be some adults with whom they do not get along – it happens in the outside world, too, so let's prepare them for such an event.

Use circle time to discuss 'what-if' scenarios and get the children to share their ideas about handling situations such as the following.

● You feel a teacher is picking on you – what do you do?
● You find one subject really boring because the teacher just talks at you – what do you do?
● You like to discuss with a group to help you with your learning but the teacher insists that you work in silence – what do you do?
● You are finding the work too hard – what do you do?

Invite the children to come up with their own scenarios for discussion. If they share their fears with their peers, they will probably find that others share those fears with them and they can support each other through the process of transfer.

Preparing the secondary school for your pupils

How are the secondary schools going to react to pupils who understand themselves as learners and have been used to having a level of autonomy in their learning? Hopefully, they will be working towards developing PL in their school, too, and will welcome independent thinkers; but, just in case they aren't quite up to your speed, how do you bring them on board?

First, make links – probably the head of Year 7 is your first point of contact, but try to make links with the curriculum deputy headteacher too.

● Invite them to attend your meeting for parents that explains your approach to learning.
● Invite them to visit your classrooms and watch children at work.
● Invite them to talk to your children about their development as independent learners.
● Invite them to talk to your Year 6 pupils about their school's expectations of them in Year 7.
● Provide time for the Years 6 and 7 teachers to meet to discuss the children.

Transfer of information

Another key aspect to consider would be the transfer of information to the secondary school about individual pupils, not in terms of administrative data – that is covered by the pupil-transfer forms – but in terms of pupils as individual learners.

What better way than to get the children to write about themselves? It is a very good activity for Year 6 pupils following their SATs. They could use the information about their key skill development from their PEPI pack and have a cover sheet with a personal profile (similar to the starting-school profile that they completed during the home visit before they began nursery or reception class). An example is provided in Figure 7.1.

My favourite ways of learning are:
My least favourite ways of learning are:
I am good at:
I need help with:
My interests and hobbies are:
I belong to the following organisations/clubs:
The musical instrument I play is:
I have represented my school in borough activities for:
My contribution to my primary school was:
My hopes for my secondary education are:
My fears of secondary education are:

Figure 7.1 A typical personal-profile cover sheet

This sort of paper exercise does not, of course, take the place of first-hand experience. It would be hoped that you can work closely with your secondary school(s) to facilitate visits for staff and pupils to ease the worry of transition.

Here are some ideas that you might want to pursue.

- Meet with the head of Year 7 at your link secondary schools.
- Invite the head of Year 7 to visit your school, regularly.
- Arrange for your Year 6 pupils to spend some time at your link secondary schools to use specialist facilities.
- Invite the Head of Year 7 to meet with your Year 6 parents.
- Introduce a transition project – a piece of work that the children begin at the end of the summer term in Year 6 and continue in the autumn term in Year 7.
- Arrange for Year 7 pupils to come back and talk to your Year 6 pupils about their experience of starting secondary school.
- Make connections with your link secondary schools' sixth forms and see if they would be interested in becoming learning mentors to Year 6 pupils at your school.

Of course, the ideal solution to the issues surrounding transfer from primary to secondary school is not to have it. If we get PL right in the primary sector and look at the possibilities afforded by extending it to include Year 9, then pupils will be in a much better position to make decisions about their future pathways, whether it be in transferring to further or higher education institutions for further academic learning or to apprenticeships in the community for vocational training or a mixture of both.

CHAPTER 8

Leading a Personalising Learning School

As a headteacher

If you are a headteacher who's keen on introducing personalising learning into your school, you will, eventually, have to review policy and practice in all areas of the school. You will need to look at:

● the school's ethos, culture and values;
● finance and resourcing policy and practice;
● staffing policy;
● curriculum provision, including the learning environment;
● learning and teaching policy and practice;
● external relations policy and practice; and
● the review, monitoring and evaluation policy and practices.

All of these areas will have some impact on your plans to introduce PL, so your review of current practice will help give you focus about where you will need to begin. Some aspects can be adapted quite easily, while others will take further deliberation and shifts in the school culture.

Figure 8.1 illustrates a mind map that shows some of the issues that will need consideration under each of the above headings.

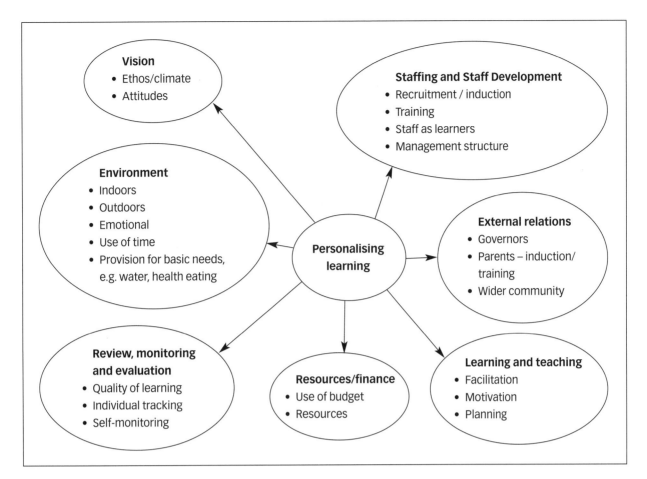

Figure 8.1

At this stage, your deliberations will be done either independently or with a small group of people who, I would suggest, should include at least your deputy and your chair of governors. You will probably want to make contact with and visit schools that have begun on the journey to personalising the curriculum. There are several case studies on the DfES Standards website, www.standards.dfes.gov.uk/personalisedlearning.

Before embarking on your journey with your whole staff, there are a number of issues that you would want to consider. I would suggest that you start by sharing the review of your current position. Sharing your Ofsted self-evaluation form (SEF) with your senior management team and/or governing body would be a good place to begin. Once you have shared your completed and evidenced SEF, together you can undertake a SWOT analysis (see Figure 8.2) to help you consider some of the **s**trengths, **w**eaknesses, **o**pportunities and **t**hreats to taking personalising learning on board.

Strengths	**Weaknesses**
What are the positives about adopting PL in your school?	What are the negatives about adopting PL in your school?
Opportunities	**Threats** (political, economic, social and technological)
What could be the benefits of adopting PL in your school?	What could be the potential threats in adopting PL in your school?

Table 8.1 SWOT analysis

CHECKLIST

Here is a checklist of issues to consider when undertaking your SWOT exercise:

● What do your pupils think about their learning? Are they excited about coming to school every day?
● What is the morale of your staff like? Are they open to change? Will they be excited about learning more about learning?
● What do your parents and governors think about personalising learning? How do you know?
● Is there already practice in place that would support your implementation of personalising learning?
● Is there an open, honest, trusting culture of teamwork in your school?
● Do you have the capacity at this time to make the necessary changes?
● Do you know enough about PL to lead the changes yourself or do you need support from elsewhere?

If you are convinced that the time is right and that you will have a high level of support from your staff, governors and parents, where do you begin?

I am not advocating that you should throw out your current practice and start building a PL school from scratch. The first thing to do is find out exactly what is happening in your school and whether it is good practice in terms of supporting effective learning for all of your pupils. You can do this through classroom

	QUESTION	YES	NO	OTHER RESPONSE
1	Do you like coming to school?			
2	Do you enjoy learning?			
3	Are you good at learning?			
4	How do you know?			
5	Does your teacher help you if you get stuck?			
6	Are you always encouraged to improve your learning?			
7	Does your teacher like to listen to your ideas?			
8	Does your teacher sometimes let you choose which work you do?			
9	Does your teacher sometimes let you choose who you work with?			
10	Is there anything else you would like to say about your school or your learning?			

Figure 8.2 A pupil questionnaire

	QUESTION	YES	NO	OTHER RESPONSE
1	Do you think that your child is treated as an individual?			
2	Do you think that your child is encouraged to do their best?			
3	Do you feel well informed about your child's progress?			
4	Do you know who to talk to if you have concerns about your child's progress?			
5	Do you know what your child is learning at school?			
6	Do you know how to help your child with their learning at home?			
7	Do you know whom to talk to if you are unsure about helping your child at home?			
8	Does your child like school?			
9	Do you think that your child's individual talents are being developed?			
10	Any other comments about the school's approach to learning:			

Figure 8.3 A questionnaire for parents

observations and questionnaires to pupils, parents and staff, and start discussions about what makes learning effective during staff meetings. Figures 8.2 to 8.5 are examples of questionnaires and classroom observation schedules that you could use.

This first questionnaire (Figure 8.2) could be used with children from Year 2 upwards, though you may wish to read the questions out to the younger ones and explain them if children are unsure. I would suggest that you ask that the responses be anonymous by not asking for names to be written on the form, but ask the children to write on the top which year group they are in and whether they are a boy or a girl. This may provide you with some interesting comparative data. A questionnaire for parents is given as Figure 8.3.

As a piece of real-life data-analysis work, the Year 6 pupils could be given the task of collating the information and presenting a report on their findings of the views of parents and pupils.

You will also want to check on the opinions of staff too (Figure 8.4).

Questionnaires should be distributed to all staff who are engaged in supporting learning, regardless of their status. Again, you will want to receive anonymous responses so that people feel that they can respond truthfully. You will want to analyse the results from the staff questionnaire yourself or with your senior management team.

As well as questionnaires, you will also want to investigate current learning and teaching practice within your classrooms. Figure 8.5 shows an example of a classroom observation pro forma that focuses on the quality of learning rather than the quality of teaching. Record your observations on the children engaged

	QUESTION	YES	NO	OTHER RESPONSE
1	Do you feel that you are treated as an individual?			
2	Do you feel that you treat pupils as individuals?			
3	Do you encourage pupils to be actively involved in planning their own learning?			
4	How?			
5	Do you encourage pupils to be actively involved in assessing their own learning?			
6	How?			
7	Do you encourage pupils to learn collaboratively?			
8	How?			
9	Do you encourage parents to support their child's learning?			
10	How?			
	Any other comments:			

Figure 8.4 A questionnaire for staff

in learning activities and provide feedback to the team of adults facilitating learning within that classroom. Consider together ways forward and record these on the form – in this way you could highlight aspects of practice that could contribute to your move towards personalising learning.

Once you have this baseline of feedback from pupils, parents and staff, you can begin to have discussions with staff about developing personalising learning in your school.

In a staff meeting, ask them to reflect upon the most memorable learning experiences from their own school days. At a guess, I think very few of them will remember an exciting worksheet. Their memories will be linked to times of extreme emotion, either positive or negative, or to the unusual or memorable, such as a field trip or a school production.

You can then encourage them to think about the learning experiences of the pupils in their classes. You can get them involved in undertaking some reflective exercises, for example, keeping a log of what the children actually do during the day – is it all listening to the teacher and then going to do what you have been told, which is usually going to your table and engaging in solo writing activities?

If they are a confident staff, where there are trusting relationships, get them to observe each other and provide factual feedback of what they saw the children doing during a session.

Encourage them to use the Open University six questions from the *Curriculum in Action* pack (1980):

Class:

Date:

Teacher:

Support Staff:

QUESTION	EXPECTATIONS	EVIDENCE FROM OBSERVATION
What did the pupils actually do?	• Clear learning objectives for pupils and shared with them. • Differentiated learning? • Work which is challenging but not beyond reach.	
How did the pupils respond?	• Independence • Interest, motivation, involvement • Confidence • Relationships • On-taskness • Behaviour • Collaboration • Use of skills	
What progress have the pupils made?	• New skills and ideas • Revision and consolidation of new learning • Progressive improvement	
To what extent are pupils involved in assessing their progress?	• Pupils' understanding of the assessment criteria • Pupils' views on progress valued • Value placed on individual achievement • Next steps discussed	
Any other observations of a significant nature		

Teaching and learning styles:

Whole class	Mixed-ability groups	Ability groups	Pairs	Individual
Teacher-led	Explaining	Instructing	Demonstrating	Questioning
Observing	Assessing	Diagnosing	Providing feedback	Child-led

Key issues for feedback:	Ways Forward:	Signed:

Figure 8.5 An example of an observation pro forma to record learning and teaching practices

1 What did the pupils actually do?
2 What were they learning?
3 How worthwhile was it?
4 What did I do?
5 What did I learn?
6 What do I intend to do now?

Encourage further reflection on action by asking for an evaluation of the previous week's learning as part of their weekly planning sheets. This can be done on a blank sheet of paper attached to the plans or can be part of the planning sheet; but staff should reflect on the quality of learning outcomes from the previous week in terms of what worked for which children and why. They should be encouraged to be as specific as possible in their reflections and not provide you with bland comments such as 'this activity went well'.

Planning meetings held for year groups or departments should also include some reflective activity around the quality of learning.

In addition to encouraging your staff to become reflective practitioners, you will also want to be sure that all your staff hold the same understanding about what personalising learning will look like in your school. This cannot at any stage be a definitive discussion, because personalising learning is a journey, not a destination, but it will at least ensure that you are all beginning to develop a shared understanding.

You can begin by asking staff to consider what an independent learner looks like, otherwise how will they know how to help children develop their independence? One way to reach this level of agreement is to hold a debate with your staff during a staff meeting or INSET day on the qualities and learning behaviours an independent learner would exhibit at different ages and stages within your school.

Staff can work together in their year groups or departments (Foundation Stage, Key Stage 1, Lower Key Stage 2 and Upper Key Stage 2) and mind-map around the question: What does an independent learner look like in your year group or department (at age 4, 7, 9 and 11)? Once each team has completed its mind map, you can bring them together and look at continuity and progression in developing independence across the school, so that everyone develops understanding of the full picture from 4 to 11. This discussion should lead to an agreement on expectations in each department or year group. You can then move on to talk about how this is reflected in practice, i.e. what it looks like. This will then lead you into discussions around the kind of learning environment and learning experiences that will need to be provided if children are to develop their independence.

In this way you are setting up whole-school approaches to developing independent learners, and, because the thinking has come from the staff, they will be more likely to implement what they have agreed.

Other ways of getting started

You can:

● provide some exciting inputs on INSET days to whet the appetite and inspire your staff (if you can't afford to buy in an inspirational speaker on your own, band with other local schools around you and share the cost);

- reproduce articles for staff to read;
- take them on visits to other schools that have already started to be innovative in developing effective learning practices and learn from their learning;
- encourage staff to take on mini action-research projects in their classrooms and report to each other on the outcomes of their learning about learning;
- buy books to build up a staff library to be used as reference and for ideas;
- make links with your local higher-education institutions to see how they are engaged with learning about learning; and
- search the Web for information to display for staff.

There are lots of ways to begin. It is up to you to decide what would be the right approach for you and your staff, given your current context. My advice would be to start small and build on your success in developing personalising learning gradually. You are trying to shift attitudes and values and this takes time.

CAUTION

- It will take a 'mature' staff team to start to question what they do and why they do it that way and be willing to change quite radically, but, once they see the benefits of motivated learners, they too will become motivated to 'risk' a little more.
- It's not going to be an easy journey. You will be destabilising your organisation, so will need to be ready to catch people as they 'wobble', providing reassurance and support as necessary. You will need to show that you are the lead learner in your institution and lead by example by always reflecting on your practice and trying to improve it. There will be lots of moments of excitement during your journey but there may also be times of great despair when you think you are making no progress at all. That is the time to stop and take stock, marking out the milestones you have achieved on your way and refocus for your future journey.

Once you have got the staff enthused about trying out new things in their classrooms and sharing their reflections on the outcomes, you will need to begin that systematic review of all your policies and practices to ensure that they support your approaches to learning.

You will need to take a close look at your written policies and make sure that they reflect and underpin your new approaches. Consider the following:

- your school mission statement;
- your school aims;
- your finance and resourcing policy, which should reflect that you are maximising finance for personnel and purchasing resources that can be used flexibly;
- your staffing policy and practice, which should:
  - reflect that you will be looking to employ staff who have a commitment to learning about learning;
  - include your commitment to the induction of staff and provide an outline of your induction plans; and
  - include a review of your interview questions to ensure that you are able to elicit new staff's philosophy on learning;

- your learning environment, which will include a review of:
  - the creation of the right kind of emotional environment;
  - the space for learning – indoors and outdoors;
  - the kind and amount of furniture you provide;
  - the time for learning; and
  - the meeting of children's physical needs;
- your curriculum provision, which should include:
  - what your curriculum should look like;
  - the enrichment of your curriculum; and
  - your extended curriculum provision;
- your learning and teaching policy, which will reflect your shared values;
- your external relations, including:
  - your work with parents;
  - your links with the community;
  - your links with other schools; and
  - your links with the LEA, DfES, or other local or national government agencies;
- your review, monitoring and evaluation policy, which will include:
  - how you engage pupils in review;
  - how you encourage staff to evaluate their practice; and
  - how you monitor for quality learning.

In the Appendices I have included some examples of policies, interview questions, schedules, etc. that you may find useful as a beginning of your discussions with your staff and governors.

As a class teacher

If you are a class teacher interested in developing personalising learning and you are a lone voice in your school, where do you begin? I would suggest that you begin by analysing your current practice.

- Are there aspects of your practice that you want to improve in order to benefit the learners in your class?
- Are there aspects of your current practice that cause you concern in terms of effective learning for your pupils?
- Are there aspects of your current practice that excite and motivate you?
- Are there things that you are keen to try out?
- Do you know what constitutes effective learning for each individual in your class?

Once you have a clear idea about the direction in which you would like to develop your practice, begin by planning small steps. Pick one idea that you will implement over a defined period and see what happens. If you are working with a teaching assistant or other adult support in your classroom, involve them in your 'research'. Ask them if they have noticed any changes in the children's learning behaviours since you have worked in this new way. Ask the children for feedback on what they think about your new approaches.

As you begin to see results and gather evidence about your success in this area, you might want to share it with others in your year group or department. You can talk to your colleagues about it during your planning meetings and invite them to come to your classroom to see the changes for themselves. They may even be interested enough to try things out for themselves in their classrooms if they see your success.

When you are feeling confident about the success of your approaches, discuss them with your line manager and your senior management team, perhaps as part of your performance review interview. Provide them with background information and research around the area of practice that you have adopted and let them know how things have been going in your classroom.

Inform them that several of your colleagues have shown an interest in your approach and would welcome further input or training so that they can adopt the practices themselves. Suggest a speaker who could be asked to provide INSET for staff or printed material in the form of articles that could be circulated for information. In this way you are becoming a catalyst for change within your own institution. If enough of your colleagues want to work in this new way, senior management would be foolish to ignore it.

Of course, sometimes you will come up against a brick wall, where no one in your school is interested in your 'new-fangled ideas about learning'. In these circumstances, you will have to make a choice – do I stay where I am and look for support outside the school, or do I move to another school where I will be supported in developing myself as a reflective practitioner?

If you choose to stay in your current school and look for support externally, you could:

- make links with friends or colleagues in other local schools and share your ideas and practice with them;
- make contact with your local adviser or school-improvement partner, who may well know of others schools or individual teachers working on similar approaches and contact them;
- contact your local professional development centre and see if they provide training in your area of interest or if there are networks of schools in your area working on personalising learning;
- search on the Web for schools in your locality that are working on personalising learning and see if you can visit; and/or
- contact your local higher-education institution and see if they make provision for teachers who want to study at postgraduate level – you may even choose to enrol yourself on a master's degree programme and formalise your research.

Eventually, though, if you choose to stay in your current school, you will find that your level of dissatisfaction will only deepen. There will come a time when you will have to make a choice as to whether you remain in a school that is not allowing you to grow personally or professionally. In these circumstances, I would suggest that the only choice left open to you is to move schools.

CHAPTER 9

Out-of-School Learning

UNDERNEATH THIS FACADE I'M
WRITING MY FIRST NOVEL!

Working with parents and children 0–3

As we saw earlier, children arrive at school at the age of three or four with a wealth of previous learning experience, whether they have been at home with a parent or carer or in pre-school provision.

Usually, parents are the first and best teachers their child will ever have and most are anxious to do the best for their child, ensuring that their child has the best start in life. But many are unsure how to support their child in their learning and lack confidence in their abilities as co-educators, particularly if they had a bad experience of the education system themselves.

If you are taking personalising learning on board, you will want to ensure that learning is expanded beyond the school walls and the confines of the school day, to ensure that learning happens wherever the child is. This will mean working closely with parents as co-educators and supporting them in their role.

We have already spoken about how you can keep parents fully informed about the learning that is taking place in school, by ensuring that your plans are displayed for their information, that topic information sheets are sent home regularly and that meetings are held by the teachers for cohorts of parents on a regular basis to discuss planned learning. But how do you go about encouraging them to continue to support the development of their child as a learner at home?

One way is to provide information pamphlets about various aspects of learning, which include examples of activities that can be done at home. Some examples are given in Figure 9.1.

These pamphlets can be launched at regular learning workshops for parents, where the school's approach to learning can be explained, and where parents can 'have a go' at a range of activities that their child will be engaging in at school and get ideas for activities to do at home.

One resource that we recommended to parents to support them in their role as co-learning facilitators was a book written by Bill Lucas and Alistair Smith called *Help Your Child to Succeed* (2002). It is full of handy hints and tips for parents to support their children as learners in a fun and interactive way.

If you are going to offer parents the opportunity to attend these workshops, you will need to consider when they are held. Maybe you should consider offering them at different times of the day so that more parents can attend. If the parents become engaged in learning about their child as a learner, they can be encouraged to keep a learning diary in which they record observations of their child's learning behaviours displayed at home. Discussion of parents' observation diaries and observations undertaken at school by staff forms a very powerful agenda for parent–teacher consultation meetings.

In addition to working with parents of the children you already have on roll at your school, you may also wish to provide support for younger siblings, too. This can be done in several ways.

- Offer 'stay-and-play sessions' in the Foundation Stage so that parents and younger siblings can stay at school on certain days and join in the fun with their older brothers and sisters in the nursery and reception classes.
- Start a toy library at your school, so that toddlers can come along for one session a week for a play session and borrow toys and equipment to use at home.
- Offer play sessions for babies and toddlers and their parents or carers.

You will need to consider who is going to work with the babies and toddlers and their parents.

Some schools have a teacher who is responsible for parental involvement, some delegate the function to the Foundation Stage staff in the nursery or reception classes, and some have employed a person or team of people specifically for that purpose, particularly where the school has an integrated children's centre on site.

At our school, we appointed a full-time community nursery nurse whose role was to initiate the home–school relationships through working with pre-school children and their parents or carers. She began the relationship with these families shortly after the birth of the child. She had regular contact with the local health visitors and baby clinics. As a school, we provided workspace and training to support her in her role. Following her attendance at a baby-massage course, she established a baby-massage class to enable parents to bond with their baby through physical contact. The class proved to be very popular with the parents (and the babies) and was always well attended.

She also offered music and art sessions for babies and toddlers (and their parents or carers) and these sessions were also well attended. During the sessions

The importance of music

- Music is a powerful, unique form of communication that can change the way pupils feel, think and act.
- It brings together intellect and feelings and enables personal expression, reflection and emotional development.
- As an integral part of culture, past and present, it helps pupils understand themselves and relate to others, forging important links between home, school and the wider world.
- The teaching of music develops pupils' ability to listen to and appreciate a wide variety of music and make judgements about musical quality.
- It encourages active involvement in different forms of amateur music making, both individual and communal, developing a sense of group identity and togetherness.
- It also increases self-discipline and creativity, aesthetic sensitivity and fulfilment.

Foundation Stage

During the Foundation Stage, pupils recognise and explore how sounds can be changed, sing simple songs from memory, recognise repeated sound patterns and match movement to music.

Key Stage 1

During Key Stage 1, pupils listen carefully and respond physically to a wide range of music.

They play musical instruments and sing a variety of songs from memory, adding accompaniments and creating short compositions, with increasing confidence, imagination and control.

They explore and enjoy how sounds and silence can create different moods and effects.

Key Stage 2

During Key Stage 2 pupils sing songs and play instruments with increasing confidence, skill, expression and awareness of their own contribution to a group or class performance.

They improvise and develop their own musical compositions, in response to a variety of different stimuli with increasing personal involvement, independence and creativity.

They explore their thoughts and feelings through responding physically, intellectually and emotionally to a variety of music from different times and cultures.

The importance of ICT

- Information and communication technology (ICT) prepares pupils to participate in a rapidly changing world in which work and other activities are increasingly transformed by access to varied and developing technology.
- Pupils use ICT tools to find, explore, analyse, exchange and present information responsibly, creatively and with discrimination.
- Pupils learn how to employ ICT to enable rapid access to ideas and experiences from a wide range of people, communities and cultures.
- Increased capability in the use of ICT promotes initiative and independent learning, with pupils being able to make informed judgements about when and where to use ICT to best effect, and to consider its implications for home and work both now and in the future.

Aims and purposes

ICT teaching should offer opportunities for children to:

- develop ICT capability, including their knowledge and understanding of the importance of information and of how to select and prepare it;
- develop their skills in using hardware and software to manipulate information in their processes of problem-solving, recording and expressive work;
- develop their ability to apply their ICT capability and use ICT to support their development in language and communication, and their learning in other areas; and
- explore their attitudes towards ICT, its value for themselves, others and society, and their awareness of its advantages and limitations.

What can we do at home?

You do not need to have a computer at home to support children's developing understanding of the uses of ICT.

At home they can:

- have contact with, and discussion of, the technology in their everyday environment, e.g. washing machines, televisions, videos, games consoles, hairdryers, remote-control toys, traffic lights, cash registers;
- use toys that stimulate real-life applications of ICT, e.g. telephones and cameras and ICT-based toys and games such as keyboards that can save and play back tunes, sound-activated toys, robots, walking dolls;
- talk about computers that they have used, how they made them work, what they used them for and how they knew that those tools were computers;
- develop eye–hand coordination; and
- know how to use technology safely and sensibly, e.g. not touching the plugs and switches.

If you do have access to a computer at home:

- encourage your child to use a range of programs so that they have experience and can develop expertise in word processing, data handling, the use of spreadsheets and the use of the Internet for research.

Figure 9.1 Examples of information pamphlets

the member of staff models good activities that parents can carry on at home and insists that parents take an active role during the sessions so that the babies and toddlers get the most out of the activities. She also talked informally to parents about concerns or issues arising for them and they readily asked for advice, and so they offered support to each other.

Every Friday afternoon she operated a toddler club that was well attended. Parents and children could stay and play all afternoon and, if you have the capacity, at the end of the session parents could borrow toys, games or activities to use at home. This activity was supported through fundraising activities run by the toddler group's parents themselves. For example, they held a weekly raffle and made small contributions to the cost of refreshments. The only cost to the school was the loss of the use of a small hall for one afternoon a week – a small price to pay for the links it made to the local community.

She also provided a support group for parents of pupils who had special educational needs. This was particularly well received by these parents, who commented that the group provided them with much-needed support, making them realise that they were not battling alone against the bureaucratic systems that they had encountered since the birth of their child. They would often invite their child's support worker to attend the meetings, too, so that they could discuss the learning approaches being used with their child.

Although we began all of these sessions for parents with children already in the school, they were eventually opened up to other members of our local community. We even began to receive referrals from the local health visitors and baby clinics, who were aware of families in our community who were in need of support. In this way we were developing our multi-agency working to provide support to the vulnerable families in our community.

This work with the pre-school children and their families established a partnership in education right from the very beginning. Parents began to trust their own knowledge and judgements about their children as valid and their confidence in parenting grew as a consequence. This work contributes enormously to the personalising-learning agenda, because it is a way of convincing the parents of the efficacy of looking at their children as individual learners. It extends the PL agenda beyond the school boundaries and ensures that the parents, teachers and pupils are working together for the same aim.

Working with parents takes up a lot of staff time but it is certainly worthwhile. The spin-off for the children is in having parents who understand them as learners and can therefore contribute more effectively to learning that takes place outside of the school day. The spin-off for school staff is that they have children in their class who are motivated learners and staff develop close working relationships with the parents. This facilitates honest discussion, which can often save unnecessary confrontation.

With the proposed expansion of early years' provision and the increase in the number of integrated children's centres, some schools are developing their work with the under-threes and their families. This work with the under-threes is being supported by the 'Birth to Three Matters' framework. The purpose of the framework is to provide support, information, guidance and challenge for all those with responsibility for the care and education of babies and children from birth to three years old.

The framework provides a solid foundation on which to build your PL agenda. It talks about:

- valuing and celebrating babies and children;
- recognising their individuality, efforts and achievements;
- recognising that all children have from birth a need to develop, learning through interaction with people and exploration of the world around them; and
- recognising the holistic nature of development and learning.

In the principles that underpin the framework, it talks about:

- babies as competent learners from birth;
- learning as a shared process;
- adults counting more than resources and equipment;
- routines and schedules that must flow with the child's needs; and
- children learning when they are given appropriate responsibility, being allowed to make errors, decisions and choices and being respected as autonomous and competent learners.

If you have the capacity to work with children from birth to three and their families, you will be creating a solid foundation on which to continue to build your personalising-learning agenda.

CHAPTER 10

Troubleshooting

There will be many times on your journey towards personalising learning that you will be asked questions about your approach sometimes by other people, but mainly from yourself. Below, I provide some suggested answers to some of those questions based on my own experience of building a school on the principles of personalising learning.

Questions from headteachers

Question: How can I afford to work towards personalising learning? It seems to be very expensive in terms of staffing.

Answer: If you adopt PL practices within your school, you will of course want to review your current spending profile and see where savings can be made so that more funding can be focused on appointing quality learning facilitators at teacher and teaching assistant levels.

My experience was that our supply budget was much reduced, partly because of the way we had set up our teams to provide inbuilt cover and flexibility (five teachers for every four classes), but partly because of the reduction in staff absence for sickness. I found that we were spending less on expensive printed schemes and photocopying as the emphasis shifted from the quantity of learning to the quality of learning. Children were shown how to be less wasteful of resources.

If your budget really does not allow you to improve your staffing levels, you can always look at alternative ways of supplementing the number of adults in classrooms through the use of students in training, parent helpers or community volunteers.

Question: My school is a very old building, with small classrooms and no additional space for learning, so how can we be expected to take personalising learning on board?

Answer: The type of building your school inhabits has very little to do with the quality of learning taking place within. It has much more to do with the positive can-do attitude and approach to any issue. If you are committed to taking personalising learning on board because you see that it has potential to improve learning outcomes for your children, then you will find a way. Don't forget to involve your staff and children in looking for creative solutions to working towards personalising learning.

Question: What will Ofsted say about our approach to the curriculum if we move away from teaching subjects?

Answer: Provided you can show coverage of the statutory programmes of study and have evidence of quality learning outcomes and can show your approach to the improvement in standards of achievement for all pupils, you have nothing to fear from Ofsted. Remember that the emphasis of the new inspection framework is about the quality of learning and accuracy in school self-evaluation.

On their visits to classrooms and in their discussions with your learners, Ofsted will find that your children and staff are confident and highly motivated. They will see that the children are engaged in meaningful learning activities and can articulate both their learning needs and their learning skills. You will be able to demonstrate clearly, through your tracking system and pupil profiles, that every child is making progress.

Question: What about national initiatives (or local ones) that tell me that we should be working in a particular way that does not fit with PL?

Answer: Not all local and national initiatives are statutory. As headteacher, you are the gatekeeper of what you and your school take on board and what you don't. Any new initiative should be measured against your values system: if the initiative supports and extends what you are already doing, it can be adopted and integrated into your curriculum. If it does not fit with your values system, you will need to be in a strong position to resist it.

If you, your staff and your governors are confident about what you teach, how you teach it and why you teach it that way, you are making your position stronger. Ensure that you are all using the same language to articulate your shared vision and values and that you have spent time rehearsing this with one another. You will then be in a much stronger position to resist these potentially 'harmful influences'.

Question: What if a member of my staff is not happy about working in this new way?

Answer: You will, of course, try to engage all of your staff in supporting you in working towards personalising learning. But, if you have just one member of staff who is unwilling to participate in developing the school's practice, then they will be feeling extremely isolated and vulnerable.

From my experience, teachers who place themselves in this position do not remain in the school for long. If they are competent teachers, I am sure that you will be happy to provide a reference for them. If the issue is one of incompetence, then you would refer to your personnel procedures for such an event.

Questions from parents

Question: What about the National Curriculum?

Answer: We have found from the audits of our provision that we are meeting the statutory requirements of the programmes of study in each of the National Curriculum subjects. There is no statutory guidance about how the National Curriculum should be taught and, through our extensive evaluation of the quality of learning, we know that the children are developing the skills of learning to enable them to access knowledge for themselves.

Question: As a parent, I am keen to know where your school is in the Key Stage 2 league tables.

Answer: At our school we have a particular philosophy and approach to learning. The league tables are only one indicator of a school's success. Here we are interested more in how each individual child is progressing with their learning, rather than where their cohort sits in the league tables. We have evidence to show that our children do well in the SATs but that is not the main driver for this school. We are much more interested in ensuring that every child has developed the skills necessary for lifelong learning.

We work in close partnership with the learner and their parents to ensure that we are all supporting the child in their development of their learning skills. We put great emphasis on ensuring that children know their own strengths and areas that need further development; they play a big part in planning and evaluating their own learning and are expected to monitor their own development, setting their own targets for improvement.

We want all of our parents to be involved as co-learning facilitators for their children in a way that enhances the children's self-esteem. There are many opportunities for you to learn more about this positive approach to learning and the role that you can play in it.

If, however, you feel uncomfortable with this approach and would be happier with a more traditional approach to education, perhaps you may want to consider placing your child at another school.

Question: My child has special educational needs. How will they fit into your way of working?

Answer: Your child will not be made to fit into our way of working. We will observe your child at their learning to discover how they like to learn best and we will build on their existing learning skills. Their programme of activities may well have to be supplemented with additional support in the areas of their need, but we will do our utmost to ensure that they are making good progress.

As the child's parents, you will be our greatest resource in terms of providing information about your child's special educational needs and we will want to work in close partnership with you to ensure that your child's needs are met at school and at home.

APPENDIX A
Annual Work Cycle for Governing Body Tasks

	FULL GOVERNING BODY	CURRICULUM PANEL		RESOURCES PANEL
AUTUMN TERM	• Nominate chair and vice-chair • Publish school plan • Renew business interest forms	• Terms-of-reference review • Nomination of chair and clerk to panel • SATs results analysis • Autumn package and • PANDA analysis		• Terms-of-reference review • Nomination of chair and clerk to panel • Health-and-safety review • Budget review
SPRING TERM	• School plan review • Agree new year working budget	• Foundation Stage profile analysis	Review of Learning to Learn methods and strategies and their impact on learning and learners	• Health-and-safety inspection • Security review • Prioritise repairs and maintenance • Review staff structure, roles and responsibilities • Budget review • New financial year budget setting • Lettings charges review
SUMMER TERM	• School plan review day • School plan presentation • Annual report agreement	• LEA annual review report • Annual parents report and planning for meeting		• Health-and-safety review • Headteacher performance review • Budget review • Annual salary reviews

APPENDIX B
Behaviour Policy

At .... School we are striving to create a happy, caring and secure environment for children and staff. This involves children and staff working together to develop a good, friendly, cooperative working relationship for the benefit of all.

We believe that education must be a partnership between the child, the home and the school, and we will endeavour to strengthen these links.

Aims

We have identified, as a staff, that we must work towards the following aims:

1 Every child should have respect for him/herself and for other people.
2 Every child should have respect for property and the environment.
3 Children should learn truth, politeness and good manners.
4 Every child should develop the ability to listen and to respect the rights and feelings of those around him/her.
5 Children should try to be tolerant and considerate in their dealings with others.
6 Every child should develop the notion of self-discipline and become a responsible member of our school and community.

Framework of our code of conduct

1 New staff should be informed of the day-to-day rules of the school, as part of their induction.
2 Each class teacher is responsible for the pastoral needs of their class.
3 The senior management team (SMT) may act in a pastoral role when the class teacher requires extra help or advice.
4 The SMT can be asked for advice in relation to a specific special educational needs issue.
5 Pastoral discussions relating to particular children may take place informally and in staff meetings.
6 Regular liaison meetings between the teaching and support staff should take place so that support staff are kept fully informed.

Golden Rules

We have adopted the Golden Rules system. The Golden Rules are:

At .... School we respect each other
1 Do be gentle: Don't hurt anyone.
2 Do be kind: Don't hurt other people's feelings.
3 Do be honest: Don't hide the truth.
4 Do look after property: Don't waste or damage it.

5 Do listen well: Don't interrupt.

6 Do work hard: Don't waste your time or others' time.

Treat others as you would like to be treated.

The Golden Rules are applied everywhere: in the school, in the street, in the home, in the community. Golden Rules are rules for life.

Children are expected to abide by the Golden Rules – if they do, they are entitled to twenty minutes per week (Golden Time) to choose their activity, which could be:

● a favourite game or activity in the classroom;

● working in another classroom with a different class; or

● work shadowing a member of the office staff, site management staff or head or deputy head.

If children do not apply the Golden Rules, the member of staff will take a minute off their Golden Time for that week. The class teacher should be kept informed of any minutes lost so that they can be recorded.

In order to learn forgiveness, children should be given the opportunity to 'earn' back lost minutes – these can be returned only by the adult who took the minute(s) initially.

Awards and praise

We aim, as a staff, to be positive in our approach to the question of behaviour. Awards and praise play a large part in school life.

Awards and praise used by staff fall into the following categories:

1 stickers for individuals or classes;

2 letters home to parents;

3 achievement assembly;

4 immediate praise from the class teacher and/or other colleagues; and

5 displays of good work inside and outside the classroom.

Sanctions

Infringements of the rules may involve:

1 further explanation to the child of the reasons for the rule;

2 separating the child from the scene of disruption – sending them to the team leader initially, with the deputy headteacher and headteacher to be used, as appropriate;

3 apologies to individuals;

4 loss of privileges, e.g. missing trips (if their attendance would endanger others and if the sanction does not interfere with the delivery of the curriculum) or parties;

5 temporary or permanent confiscation of questionable articles; and/or

6 consultation with parents, which can take place at any of the above stages.

Persistent offences of a serious nature may well lead to exclusion.

Recording of incidents

A book will be kept for the recording of incidents in the school, and another book for accidents and first aid treatment undertaken.

Curriculum and other activities

It is important that each child be stimulated by a wide and interesting curriculum. We aim to develop and encourage positive attitudes such as cooperation, consideration and tolerance within our school. These attitudes may be reinforced and developed during assemblies, class times and extracurricular activities.

Bullying

Bullying may be defined as the abuse of power by an individual or group in relation to another individual or group. It may occur frequently or infrequently, regularly or irregularly, but it should be taken seriously, even if it has occurred on only one occasion. (Racism is a form of bullying.) It can be:

● physical aggression, actual or threatened;
● the use of putdown comments or insults, e.g. with regard to another child's family;
● name calling;
● damage to the person's property or work;
● deliberate exclusion from activities; and
● the setting up of humiliating experiences.

Central to the definition of bullying are the intent and motivation of the perpetrator, which will primarily be to exert power over another in order to cause distress.

Bullying is not a phenomenon that occurs solely between children. The above definition can also be seen to characterise some adult–adult, adult–child and child–adult relationships.

In more serious instances the abuse of power by an adult over a child, or by a child over a child, may be viewed as child abuse and bullying should be seen within this context. In these circumstances child-protection procedures will be appropriate.

The staff at .... **School are firmly committed to stamping out acts of bullying.**

Allegations of bullying are taken seriously and investigated by the head-teacher.

Victims of bullying will be supported. No one deserves to be bullied, even if his or her behaviour is irritating or annoying.

Through the curriculum, activities are planned to develop positive relationships and to discuss issues associated with bullying.

Sanctions will be applied to incidents of bullying as to other incidents, with exclusion as the ultimate sanction.

This code of conduct and discipline is the responsibility of every adult who works in the school. We should try to be as consistent as possible in the way we use the code.

Monitoring and evaluation

The policy will be regularly monitored and evaluated annually as part of the School Development Planning processes.

APPENDIX C
Evaluation Policy

Rationale

To provide an evaluative framework that will enable all members of staff and governors to ensure quality of provision at .... School.

Aim

To enable us to improve the quality of education provided for our pupils.

Purposes of evaluation

Evaluation should lead to judgements, which should be acted upon and incorporated into subsequent evaluation processes. These judgements should be based upon a full range of evidence, including a variety of performance indicators, such as Key Stages 1/2 data, attendance rates and budget data:

- to establish the extent to which the educational needs of our children are being met;
- to improve the quality of learning and teaching and the standards of achievement;
- to recognise, identify and share effective practice within our school;
- to enable all staff to become more effective;
- to ensure the most effective and efficient use of resources;
- to ensure accountability at all levels;
- to inform policy, planning and developments within the school; and
- to identify future resource needs.

Principles

We believe that both individuals and the school can learn and that enhancing the quality of learning for both will lead to greater effectiveness.

The learning gained from evaluation exercises must feedback directly into the planning cycle in order to maximise the use of evaluative material for improvement.

Evaluation data and judgements should be used at a strategic level where appropriate to inform policy development, resource allocation and future planning for the school.

We promote high standards of achievement for all – using our definition of achievement as stated in our Teaching and Learning Policy.

Clear and accessible systems for reporting and communication are central to effective implementation of this policy.

All staff should be involved in self-review. The outcomes of such exercises can be discussed with the headteacher as part of the professional development interviews.

Evaluation processes at .... School

Individual

Through their professional development interview and also through their membership of their year team and department team, staff are encouraged to review, monitor and evaluate their practice within a supportive framework.

Year team/department team

Each team should have a weekly meeting, where it is able to review its work and redefine its planning.

Department teams will be used for whole-school planning and review as part of our school development plan working practices.

Senior management team

Weekly meetings will be held to evaluate the work of the school and to assist forward planning.

Whole school

An annual meeting will be held for the specific purpose of reviewing and prioritising future work as part of the school development planning process. Governors will be invited to attend this meeting.

A programme of staff meetings will be developed, some of which will be used to monitor and evaluate work in progress and discuss ways forward.

All school policies include a statement about their review, monitoring and evaluation procedures.

Working definitions

Review

Answers the question, 'What are we currently doing?'.

It is a retrospective activity (unlike monitoring, which is ongoing). It is about the collection and assessment of a whole range of information (including perceptions, opinions and judgements) relating to a particular programme, initiative, provision, etc. A review process will often be followed by evaluative judgements about the quality of what has been reviewed.

Monitoring

Answers the question, 'Are we doing what we say we are doing?'.

It is concerned with the systematic, regular gathering of information about the *extent* to which agreed or required plans, policies or statutory requirements are being implemented.

Evaluation

Answers the question: 'What is the *worth* of what we do?'.

Evaluation is the general term to describe any activity where the *quality* of provision is the focus of systematic study. It involves the making of *judgements*, usually based on evidence collected by review and monitoring processes.

APPENDIX D
External-Relations Policy

We believe that it is important to have an external relations policy because:

Aim

We want our school to respond to the changing needs of our community in order to maximise the educational opportunities for our pupils.

Objectives

- to develop a positive relationship with our community;
- to develop the role of the school as a community school; and
- to strengthen the school as a community.

The policy should strengthen the school as a community by nurturing allies and friends.

KEY STAKEHOLDERS	AIMS
Parents	• To develop partnership between home and school for the ultimate benefit of the pupils • To develop the parents' role as co-educators • To generate and foster future client group
Governors	• To develop good working relationships with the governing body in order to ensure accountability
Neighbours and community	• To promote a positive image for the school and generate support locally
Partnership or network schools	• To share workload, resources and good practice
Further and higher education	• To provide staff-development opportunities • To promote quality training
Business community	• To generate links for resources and curriculum enrichment
LEA/council	• To work in partnership with LEA in order to formulate and deliver local policy • To be aware of local initiatives in which school could be involved
Professional agencies	• To support the needs of children and their families
DfES	• To manage national initiatives more efficiently
European and world links	• To promote new educational opportunities for all • To share educational practice

APPENDIX E
Finance and Resources Management Policy

Rationale

To formulate a policy that promotes an efficient and equitable use of resources by establishing rules and procedures that are recognised and accepted by everyone, to meet the stated needs of the school.

Purposes

- to provide a framework to enable the governors to meet their statutory obligations with regard to the management of the school budget;
- to provide a framework that assists and supports the prioritisation of needs and allocation of resources;
- to ensure that optimum benefit is derived from the school's budget and resources; and
- to ensure that all parties are clear about their roles and responsibilities with regard to the budgetary processes and know their lines of accountability.

Broad guidelines

- to ensure there is sufficient staffing to provide for learning and management needs;
- to ensure the efficient and effective allocation of resources throughout the school in line with stated priorities;
- to ensure the efficient and effective management of budget and resources by the establishment of appropriate committees;
- to provide effective systems for budget monitoring, with regular meetings of and reports to the finance and resources panel and full governing body; and
- to provide clear financial regulations for the internal management of finance and resources, which meet the requirements of the auditors.

This policy needs to be read in the context of:

- the school plan;
- the school pay policy;
- the school staff development policy; and
- other school policies, such as learning and teaching, external relations and review, monitoring and evaluation.

Evaluation

This policy will be reviewed and evaluated as part of the annual budgetary cycle and alongside the stated aims in the school plan.

APPENDIX F
Staff Induction Policy

The process of induction

Induction is the process that enables a newcomer to become a fully effective member of an organisation as quickly and as efficiently as possible.

To do this the newcomer needs:

KNOWLEDGE: of people, routines, procedures and facts
SKILLS: professional, personal and interpersonal
ATTITUDES: an understanding of, and sympathy with, the ethos or culture of the school, and introduction to the accepted relationships with staff, pupils and parents

Induction should be specifically designed to meet the needs of all staff on being newly appointed to the school, or on change of role within the school.

Elements of induction

Pre-visit

Before taking up the appointment, the member of staff should visit the school:

● to meet the headteacher and staff;
● to gather information about the organisation of the school;
● to see policy documents and guidelines;
● to find out about resources and equipment available; and
● to discuss support, both in school and LEA provided (if any).

School programme

New members of staff should have the opportunity to:

● seek guidance from the staff development coordinator, headteacher and other staff, as appropriate;
● job-shadow other staff, if appropriate;
● visit other schools, as appropriate;
● receive advice about their own work; and
● attend central courses, as appropriate.

Mentor

The whole staff share the responsibility for the induction of new members of staff, but one person is designated as their mentor, to act as a model of good practice – to guide, advise and support.

The mentor's role should involve:

● communicating vital information about the school-based induction programme to all members of staff;

- organising the school-based programme in consultation with colleagues and making sure that it is in line with the school's policies in other areas;
- encouraging and facilitating the contribution of other colleagues in providing support for newly appointed staff; and
- coordinating aspects of induction such as links with external support systems, ensuring release to attend centrally organised sessions, etc.

Assessment procedures

The mentor will work very closely with the newly appointed member of staff to assist in self-evaluation, offer any support felt to be necessary and, for newly qualified teachers, write reports on progress, as required by the headteacher.

Newly qualified teachers should be informed at an early stage when any problems emerge that might lead to adverse assessment, be warned of any consequences and be given an opportunity to heed advice.

School plan

A significant element of the school development plan will be concerned with the induction plan in the context of professional development for all staff.

Such a programme will result in making specific arrangements for integrating new members of staff at all levels of experience into the work of the school, ensuring that they have the necessary knowledge, resources and support to enable them to contribute successfully to the work of the school.

Evaluation

The induction process will be evaluated annually to ensure that it is meeting the needs of newly appointed members of staff.

Their mentor will ask them whether their induction was successful and whether there were ways in which it could be improved.

APPENDIX G
INSET Policy

The purpose of INSET is to support school improvement and should directly relate to raising pupil achievement. This can be done by:

- encouraging staff to be engaged in the continuous process of self-evaluation, whereby they are continually reflecting on the quality of their work and their interactions with colleagues;
- giving staff the freedom and encouragement to innovate as a staff, without fear of punishment or failure;
- shared planning and evaluation;
- observing each other's performance and using each other for feedback; and
- seeking opportunities for individuals to experience leading other adults.

Training needs

Training needs should be identified as part of induction, performance management and school evaluation systems.

Staff individual needs can be met through school-based training opportunities, e.g.:

- leading staff meetings;
- preparing draft policy statements through membership of working parties;
- leading parent meetings;
- working collaboratively with other colleagues;
- job shadowing; or
- attendance at centrally run courses.

Funding of courses and cover will be maintained, as far as possible, to enable staff's learning to continue.

Not all courses that staff attend will be to support school development priorities, as we also highly value our entitlement to our own personal professional development.

Feedback from courses attended will be facilitated through staff meetings or workshops.

Evaluation

The INSET policy will be reviewed annually as part of the school development planning processes.

APPENDIX H
Performance Management Policy

Rationale

Performance management should be:

- an integral part of our school's culture;
- fair and open;
- understood by everyone;
- based on shared commitment to supporting continuous improvement; and
- central in recognising success.

This means:

raising standards: looking in the round at the way our school works to provide the best possible education for our pupils and planning the work of individual staff in that context;

continuous professional development: promoting professional growth and taking account of staff's individual development needs;

involvement: encouraging staff to be fully engaged in school planning, to control the development of their own work and to support each other;

manageability: so that performance management is regarded as an integral and essential part of how our school operates; and

equity: to ensure policies and processes are open and fair, while respecting the confidentiality of individuals.

Commitment

The senior management team are committed to agreeing, monitoring and reviewing objectives with every member of staff, on at least an annual basis.

There is a commitment to ensure that equal opportunities operate in practice.

Roles and responsibilities

All staff:

- will self-review and reflect on their practice with a view to continual improvement;
- will accept their entitlement to receive ongoing, continuing support in their own professional development and recognise the need for their active role in this;
- will accept their responsibility to take an active role in the professional development of their colleagues; and
- will take an active role in the review of this policy.

The headteacher:

- accepts responsibility to implement this policy;
- will be responsible for the day-to-day management of this policy;

- will ensure that targets are set and monitored for every member of staff;
- will ensure that individual targets are reflected in future training needs, as outlined in the school development plan;
- will be responsible for monitoring the implementation of this policy and coordinating the evaluation in collaboration with all staff and governors; and
- will ensure that monitoring of quality learning takes place and that feedback enables staff to reflect on their performance and to participate fully in the discussion.

The governing body:

- has a strategic role;
- will need to agree the school's performance management policy;
- will ensure that the policy is operating effectively; and
- has a duty to review the performance of the headteacher.

Timing of reviews/performance management cycle

The one-year performance management cycle links with our planning for school management and target setting. The governing body needs to ensure that objectives have been agreed or set for the headteacher by the end of September and for all other teaching staff by the end of October, annually.

Performance management is a process involving:

Planning: Objectives will be set for each member of staff and progress will be monitored.

Monitoring: Individual staff in collaboration with the headteacher will keep progress under review throughout the cycle, taking any supportive action needed.

Review: Individual staff in collaboration with the headteacher will review achievements over the year and evaluate overall performance taking account of progress against objectives.

The school will operate an annual cycle for performance management, but professional development interviews will be offered termly. A choice of dates and times will be offered in order to give maximum flexibility.

Staff will have the choice of the autumn or spring term to focus particularly on performance management in order to ensure that collective targets are available for the school development planning cycle.

Stage 1: Planning

Each member of staff in collaboration with the headteacher will agree the focus for performance management, for the year, at the start of the review cycle, i.e. in the autumn term.

- Each member of staff will have a clear job description. This can be the starting point for review.
- Priorities will be discussed, including the needs of the pupils and personal priorities, and specific objectives will be agreed for the coming year. Teachers' objectives will cover pupil progress as well as ways of developing and

improving teachers' professional practice. The headteacher's objectives will cover school leadership and management as well as pupil progress.

- No fewer than three objectives and no more than six will be agreed. The reviewer will record the objectives, which will apply for the review period. These should be jointly agreed if possible. If there are any differences of opinion about the objectives, the teacher may add comments to the written record of objectives. If the headteacher and the governing body representative(s) are unable to agree objectives, the governors appointed to review the performance of the headteacher should set and record the objectives. The headteacher may add comments to the written record of objectives.
- Objectives will be recorded on the professional discussion summary sheet (included at the end of this policy), a copy will be given to the member of staff to be kept in their portfolio and a copy kept by the headteacher.

Stage 2: Monitoring

Continual attention to progress made needs to be a focus throughout the year.

- Staff are encouraged to self-review and evaluate their classroom practice as part of their weekly planning; this is recorded on the planning sheets.
- The senior management team will undertake classroom observation at least twice a year. Classroom observation is accepted good practice with a minimum of one observation each year required by the regulations. It is not a requirement to observe headteachers with teaching responsibilities.
- An agreed pro forma for classroom observation will be used; a copy will be given to each member of staff to be kept in their portfolio and a copy will be kept by the headteacher.
- Feedback will be given to the staff team at the earliest opportunity following the observation, with an opportunity to discuss what went well and discuss areas for development.
- The reviewer should consult the teacher before seeking to obtain information, written or oral, relevant to the teacher's performance from other people.

Stage 3: Review

An annual review is an opportunity for staff to reflect on their performance in a structured way, to recognise and celebrate their achievements and to discuss areas for future development and training. The annual review of the teacher's performance will use the recorded objectives as a focus to discuss their achievements and identify any development needs.

The focus for review should be on how to raise performance and improve effectiveness.

- Review, discuss and confirm the member of staff's essential tasks, objectives and standards.
- Recognise the member of staff's strengths and achievements.
- Confirm action agreed during professional development interviews.
- Identify areas for development and how these needs will be met.
- Recognise personal-development needs.

Within ten days of the review meeting, the reviewer will prepare a written review statement recording the main points made at the review and the conclusions reached, including any identified development needs and activities recorded in a separate annexe. Once the review is written, the reviewer will give the teacher a copy of the statement. The teacher may, within ten days of first having access to the statement, add to it comments in writing.

Complaints procedure

Within ten days of receiving the review statement:

- Teachers can record their dissatisfaction with aspects of the review on the review statement. Where these cannot be resolved with the reviewer, they can raise their concerns with the headteacher. Where the headteacher is the reviewer, the teacher can raise the issue with the chair of governors.
- Headteachers can record their dissatisfaction with aspects of the review on the review statement. Where these cannot be resolved with the appointed governor(s), they can raise their concern with the chair of governors. Where the chair of governors has been involved in the review process, the governing body should appoint one or more governors who have not participated in the headteacher's review to act as review officer. No governor who is a teacher or staff member can be involved in performance review.
- The review officer (who could be the headteacher, the chair of governors or the governor appointed by the governing body) will investigate the complaint and take account of comments made by the jobholder. The review officer should conduct a review of the complaint within ten working days of referral. They may decide that the review statement should remain unchanged or may add any observations of their own. The review officer may decide, with the agreement of the person responsible for carrying out the initial review, or in the headteacher's case all the appointed governors, to amend the review statement, or declare that the review statement is void and order a new review or part of the review to be repeated. Where a new review is ordered, new governors will be appointed to carry out the review of the headteacher. For teachers, the headteacher will appoint a new reviewer. Any new review or part review ordered should be conducted within a further fifteen days.

Managing weak performance

Performance review does not form part of disciplinary or dismissal procedures. However, relevant information from review statements may be taken into account by those who have access to them in making decisions and in advising those responsible for taking decisions, or making recommendations about performance, pay, promotion, dismissal or disciplinary matters.

Where a decision is taken to enter into a formal capability procedure, that procedure supersedes performance management arrangements.

Access to outcomes

There will be only two copies of the review statement – one held by the teacher and another held by the headteacher on a central file, to which the reviewer or governors responsible for making decisions regarding pay could request access. A copy of the headteacher's review statement should go to the chair of governors.

Information about performance reviews should be made available as listed below.

- The headteacher should ensure that individual training and development needs are reflected in the school development plan and the programme for professional development.
- The headteacher should ensure that training and development needs from the review statement are given to the person responsible for training and development at the school.
- The headteacher should report annually to the governing body on performance management in the school, this should include the effectiveness of the performance management procedures in the school, and the training and development needs of teachers; and
- The director of education can request from the chair of governors a summary of the performance assessment section of the headteacher's review statement.

The headteacher should keep review statements for at least three years.

Review, monitoring and evaluation

The headteacher will provide an annual report to the governing body on how effective the performance management procedures have been.

This policy will be regularly reviewed and evaluated at least every two years.

Outcomes of reviews will be shared with all staff and governing body prior to any proposed changes to this policy.

Name:
Role:
Date of discussion:
Summary of discussion:
Agreed objectives / action proposals: (these can be actions to be undertaken by the mentor or mentee)
Mentor signature:
Mentee signature:

APPENDIX I
Quality Charter

At .... **School:**

- Quality learning and teaching come first.
- Staff, children, parents and governors work together.
- Everyone is special and enriches the life of our school.
- Hard work and achievements are always celebrated.
- We are kind to each other.
- We take pride in ourselves.
- We are always ready to listen.
- We make all visitors welcome.

APPENDIX J
Staff Development Policy

Rationale

All staff have an entitlement to receive continuing support in their own professional development throughout their career, and have a responsibility to take an active role in their own professional development and that of their colleagues.

This process will contribute to meeting the identified needs of the whole school, the needs of individuals and, thereby, enhance pupil achievement and the general learning environment for all.

Purposes

1 To provide the effective development of the curriculum and thus ensure continuity of teaching and learning styles.
2 To improve staff confidence, competence and self-esteem through the broadening of their experience, knowledge and skills.
3 To provide opportunities for staff to share concerns and expertise and thus develop and strengthen teams and partnerships.
4 To provide a framework for the systematic evaluation and identification of needs for the individual and the whole school, in the context of local and national initiatives.
5 To enable the school to initiate and manage change, and use time and resources efficiently and effectively.
6 To enhance personal and career development.

How?

Staff development will be facilitated through the implementation of school policies on induction, performance management and INSET.

Evaluation

The provision of staff development opportunities, both internal and external to the school, will be constantly evaluated to ensure their quality. This will be facilitated through the use of the pro forma below by all staff. The forms will be reviewed regularly by the senior management team.

Professional development evaluation form

Date(s) of course or professional development opportunity:

Course title or nature of professional development opportunity:

What were the main learning points for you from this development opportunity?

What will you do next as a consequence of your learning?

Please attach any course handouts and/or relevant notes.

APPENDIX K
Learning and Teaching Policy

Rationale

To formulate a policy, which promotes achievement in our school, by stating an entitlement, for all pupils, to a broad and balanced curriculum, which will provide opportunities for them to develop their full potential.

Aims

1 To improve the quality of learning experiences offered to pupils.
2 To clarify current practice and determine future approaches to learning and teaching.
3 To convey our basic philosophy about learning and teaching.
4 To provide an agreed framework that underpins all areas of learning.

The policy identifies the common processes of learning which inform and guide our teaching.

Review, monitoring and evaluation

Quality learning will be the focus of classroom monitoring.

Senior managers will undertake monitoring in the school and findings reported to whole staff at staff meetings. The policy will be modified, as necessary, following discussion with staff and will be presented for ratification by the governors.

Standards of achievement will be monitored by staff and governors and the learning and teaching policy evaluated in the light of statistical evidence, as necessary.

Learning

1 Pupils are entitled to have access to a wide range of learning materials, resources and real-life experiences.
2 Pupils are able to select materials and space in which to work, as appropriate to the task in hand.
3 Pupils are encouraged to take responsibility for caring for, organising and conserving learning resources in the classroom and school environment.
4 Pupils are given responsibility for organising and evaluating their learning and managing their own time.
5 Both independent and cooperative work by pupils will be facilitated and encouraged.
6 Pupils should be encouraged to ask questions and to persevere.
7 Learning activities should be planned to enable progression and to allow children to experience success.

8 The atmosphere within the school should facilitate the development of good learning attitudes that are appropriate in a variety of learning situations.

9 Pupils' specific individual interests should be valued and developed.

10 Pupils should understand that they and the school are parts of a wider community.

Teaching

Learning will be facilitated by the progressive acquisition of knowledge, skills and understanding and by:

1 using teaching techniques that make use of appropriate methods suiting the topic as well as the pupils' stage of development and preferred ways of learning;

2 lessons having clear aims and purposes as indicated in our planning, which takes into account early-learning goals, attainment targets and programmes of study of the National Curriculum;

3 teachers having high expectations of each pupil in all areas of their learning;

4 accentuating the positive in behaviour, work and attitude and by setting a good example;

5 children being involved in varying degrees with planning, organising and evaluating their own learning, e.g. they should receive regular feedback to help them progress through thoughtful marking and discussion;

6 ensuring that relationships are positive and promote pupil motivation by making pupils feel welcomed, cared for, secure and valued as individuals, by developing their self-esteem and confidence – we do this through building on strengths to promote success, regular meetings with children and parents and the use of formative feedback;

7 where appropriate, children being encouraged to engage in learning at home, which may be spellings, tables, reading activities or work that complements and extends the work done in lessons; we encourage parents to help children with their learning at home;

8 encouraging children to show concern for others and to value each person's individual contribution;

9 providing as many opportunities as possible for first-hand experience and investigative work;

10 flexible grouping strategies: children should have the opportunity to be taught in whole-class lessons, as part of a collaborative group, in pairs and individually;

11 teachers recognising that the learning process and the acquisition of skills is more important than the learning of content knowledge;

12 children having opportunities to create, express, enact, recount and communicate to others using a variety of media;

13 recognising the importance of equal opportunities, taking account of special needs, gender, race, creed and class;

14 having an approach that allows for differentiation in the curriculum, preferably by outcome, to support both the less and more able, as well as those with special needs, in a sensitive manner;

15 at all stages recognising and planning appropriate assessment and record-keeping systems that are used to guide future planning and ensure progression; and

16 the classroom and school environment being used to reflect current work themes.

Achievement

We define achievement as:

> the feeling of satisfaction and wellbeing one experiences when there has been a positive development in any aspect of learning.

The curriculum

The curriculum is regarded as the total set of learning experiences available to the learner, both in and out of the classroom. These experiences will be both planned and unplanned.

Learning should allow the pupil to link new skills, abilities, concepts and knowledge to those s/he already possesses. It follows that staff need to be aware of the point that each child has reached in his or her learning and be certain that the recording and reviewing methods employed are capable of tracking each child's progress.

Children learn most effectively when they are motivated by a sense of purpose and direction in their learning, so that, as far as practicable, they should be aware of why and how, as well as what, they are learning. They should also be involved in the decision making about their learning programmes. The way this is done will, of course, depend upon the nature and the age of the child.

School ethos

Centrally important in promoting effective learning is a positive school ethos. Every member of the school has a part to play in creating and maintaining this ethos.

Our ethos is built on the maxim that:

> all are encouraged and supported in their learning and accepted for what they are.

APPENDIX L
Assessment Policy

Assessment is a continuous process of curriculum planning, and gathering, reviewing and evaluating information in order to support children's success in their learning in all areas.

It is a key educational activity that enables us to discover a pupil's knowledge, understanding and skill development.

Methods of assessment

- Informal assessment (formative) – arising from observation of pupils, information for everyday class, and group and individual management. Informs short-term planning, which is part of the long-term assessment procedures. This can be recorded but may not be.
- Formal assessment (summative or diagnostic) – this is a more structured attempt to gather evidence and make judgements about the learning that takes place. It is used to identify specific strengths and areas for development of particular children to inform future teaching and learning. This includes formal testing as statutory requirements at the end of Key Stages. In addition, staff will assess at the end of an activity or topic and the results will be recorded in the pupils' learning profiles.
- Pupil self-assessment – pupils making decisions about their own learning. Teachers will need to acknowledge the value of their comments and judgements on their personal performance.

Purposes of assessment

- To provide information to help individuals make decisions about future learning.
- To provide information for a variety of audiences, i.e. parents, pupils, colleagues, other schools.
- To assist pupils in their learning.
- To diagnose particular difficulties that children may be encountering.
- To assist the teacher in evaluating the curriculum and their teaching.
- To motivate pupils and staff.
- To celebrate achievement by recognising children's progression.
- To comply with legal requirements.

Principles of assessment

- Assessment is an integral part of the learning process and so assessment opportunities are built in at every stage of planning the curriculum.
- Assessment takes account of every aspect of the child's development: social, emotional, physical, personal and academic, and the influence these areas have on each other.

- We have shared responsibility to ensure that:
  - (a) decisions made about children's performance are accurate, fair and consistent in practice; and
  - (b) all children have the opportunity to demonstrate their achievements.
- Reporting ensures that clear communication with parents develops an understanding of the school's practices, purposes and principles.

Working arrangements – planning for assessment

Planning is essential to effective assessment. Learning experiences are planned and an assessment of what a child *can* do within this is made.

Long term:	Topics should be planned to achieve a broad, balanced curriculum and ensure continuity and progression. Assessment opportunities and activities should be planned at this stage. End-of-Key-Stage assessments should be built into the topic grid.
Medium term:	Topic planning in year groups half-termly. Sampling of pupils work for their portfolios should be made half-termly.
Short term:	Weekly or daily planning. Clear learning objectives should be identified and assessment opportunities/activities built in. Daily observations are recorded in order to inform future planning.

Record keeping

Records supplement the teacher's personal and professional knowledge of the child. Individual running records should be kept for each child and added to as relevant, but at least half-termly.

Reporting to parents

During the summer term, teachers will draw upon their records of formal and informal assessments to prepare a summary of the child's progress enabling them to report accurately to parents.

Reporting takes place annually in July and in the context of statutory requirements. A written report is provided to parents.

In the autumn term, teachers will meet with parents to discuss the child's progress, and a written agreement of targets for the child for the coming year will be agreed between the child, parents and teacher. This written statement of targets will then be used for review purposes at subsequent consultations between teacher, child and parents.

Roles and responsibilities

Headteacher: Has overall responsibility for assessment in the school.

Assessment coordinator: Responsible for the implementation, monitoring and reviewing of assessment in the school.

Class teacher: Responsible for implementing assessment in the class.

Parents: Provide information to the school, working in partnership, being made aware of school's policy through consultation.

Governors: Make resources available to support the assessment policy and practice and have an overview of what is happening in the school through the curriculum subcommittee reports.

Pupils: Take an active part in assessment of their own learning and are encouraged to develop self-assessment skills.

Monitoring and review

The policy will be monitored by the senior management team, reviewed regularly by staff and the curriculum subcommittee of the governing body, and evaluated at least every two years as part of the school development planning processes.

APPENDIX M
Marking Strategies

(from Shirley Clarke, 2001, *Unlocking Formative Assessment*)

Summative Feedback/Marking

This usually consists of ticks and crosses and is associated with closed tasks or exercises. Wherever possible, children should self-mark or the work should be marked as a class or in a group.

Formative Feedback/Marking

With oral feedback, in the course of a lesson, teachers' comments to children should focus firstly on issues about the learning intention and, secondly, and in a whisper, on other features.

Quality Marking

Not all pieces of work can be 'quality marked'. Teachers need to decide whether work will simply be acknowledged or given detailed attention.

Wherever the task is open or narrative, feedback should focus first and foremost on the learning intention of the task. The emphasis in marking should be on both success against the learning intention and improvement needs against the learning intention. Focused comment should help the child in 'closing the gap' between what they have achieved and what they could have achieved.

With English narrative writing, codes can save time and make the feedback more accessible to the child:

- Highlight three things which are best against the learning intention.
- Put an arrow where improvement against the learning intention could take place (including a 'closing the gap' comment).

Where codes are inappropriate, success and improvement should be pointed out verbally or in written form.

Useful 'closing the gap' comments are:

- A reminder prompt (e.g. what else could you say here?)
- A scaffolded prompt (e.g. what was the dog's tail doing? The dog was angry so he … Describe the expression on the dog's face)
- An example prompt (e.g. Choose one of these or your own: He ran round in circles looking for the rabbit/The dog couldn't believe his eyes)

Secretarial Features

Spelling, punctuation, grammar, etc. should not be asked for in every piece of narrative writing, because children cannot effectively focus on too many things in one space of time. When work is finished, ask children to check for things they know are wrong in their work when they read it through. They should not be told to correct all spellings, or they are likely to write further misspellings or waste time looking words up.

Only give children feedback about those things you have asked them to pay attention to. This will mean that some aspects of writing are unmarked, but over time will be marked.

Self Marking

Children should self evaluate wherever possible. Children can identify their own three successes and look for improvement points. The plenary can then focus on this process as a way of analysing the learning.

Shared Marking

Using one piece of work from a child in another class to mark as a class, using OHP, at regular intervals, model the marking process and teach particular points at the same time.

Another strategy is to show two pieces of levelled work, with the same title, and discuss their differences.

Paired Marking

Before ends of lessons, children should sometimes be asked to mark narrative work in pairs. The following points are important:

- Paired marking should not be introduced until Key Stage 2, unless teachers feel younger children are ready for this.
- Children need to be trained to do this, through modelling with the whole class, watching the paired marking in action.
- Ground rules (e.g. listening, interruptions, confidentiality, etc.) should be decided, then put up as a poster.
- Children should, alternately, point out what they like first, holding the high-lighter pen, and then suggest ways to improve the piece, but only against the learning intention and not spellings, etc. The 3:1 success to improvement ratio should be followed, to avoid over-criticism.
- Pairings need to be based on someone you trust – best decided by teacher.
- Encourage a dialogue between children rather than taking turns to be the 'teacher'; they should discuss each other's work together (e.g. I think this bit really shows how that character feels, what do you think?).

Organisation

- The first 5–10 minutes of a lesson should, wherever possible, be used to get around the class to establish understanding and act on it where the work is too easy or too difficult.
- Where possible, children should be encouraged to self-mark.
- Set less work, so that time can be allowed to go through work and mark as a class.
- Wherever class discussions take place, feedback is given orally. Notes might also be necessary to inform future planning as a result of the discussion findings.
- Children need to have some feedback about their work, but flexibility is important, depending on the nature of the task and the time available.
- Distance marking should be accessible to children and manageable for teachers. Use codes against learning intentions wherever possible.

When work has been distance marked, time should be given for children to read and then make one focused improvement based on the improvement suggestion (linked with the arrow when codes are used). In order for the marking to be formative, the information must be used and acted on by the children.

APPENDIX N
Interview Questions

Here is a selection of questions used for selection purposes during interviews ('DHT' = 'deputy headteacher').

Deputy headteacher

- Can you give an example of a curriculum initiative that you have led through to implementation, and say how this was achieved?
- Why is collaborative management important in a school? What is the DHT's role in this?
- How do you, as DHT, ensure that the school plan is an effective document for school improvement?
- How do you ensure consistency in learning and teaching across the school?
- How can you support the involvement of parents in the education of their children?
- How do we encourage an awareness of health and safety in pupils? What is the role of staff in this?
- How do you ensure pace and challenge in your classroom?
- How would you translate teaching and learning policy into action?
- In what way can performance management support children's learning?
- What are you most proud of in relation to your current school's equal-opportunities policy?
- How will you transfer this success into practice at our school?
- What role does the DHT play in supporting staff in maintaining the ethos of this inclusive school?

Class teachers

- What do you feel are the essential elements in an effective and efficient classroom?
- How do you ensure pace and quality in your classroom?
- Tell us about any curriculum development work that you have been involved in. Why do you think it was successful?
- Describe your approach to disruptive pupils.
- How do you meet the needs of bilingual pupils in your classroom?
- What aspects of equal opportunities will you need to address in your classroom?
- A child with special needs is being admitted into your class next week – how would you go about preparing for this?
- What are your curriculum strengths?
- What areas do you feel require further development?

Nursery nurses/community nursery nurses

- What part does 'play' play in an early-years curriculum?
- How would you promote and support literacy and numeracy in the nursery?
- Can you describe a good quality outdoor curriculum?
- How would you promote links with other agencies?

- How will you ensure that your work as community nursery nurse is seen as part of whole-school developments?
- How will you work with parents to promote the role of play in learning?

Teaching assistants and learning support assistants

- How would you describe the role of the teaching assistant/learning-support assistant?
- Can you detail for us how you would support a child with a behaviour difficulty?
- Have you any experience of supporting a child with physical special needs? Could you detail for us the kind of support you provided.
- What records should be kept on children within a classroom setting?
- What sort of contact would you expect to have with parents?
- A parent comes into school at the end of the day being abusive – how would you deal with this?
- How would you communicate with a parent who spoke little or no English?
- A lot of information about the children will be confidential. How can you ensure confidentiality?
- How do you see ICT being used to support pupils' learning?
- Do you have a current first-aid certificate? When will it need to be renewed?

Support staff other than classroom assistants, e.g. site staff and administrative staff

- In a busy school office/school day, how would you go about prioritising your work?
- What computer programs have you had experience of using?
- A lot of information passing through the office will be confidential. How can you ensure confidentiality?
- Parents, staff and pupils will constantly interrupt you during the working day – how will you react to this and how will it impinge on your work?
- Why should the administrative officer, site manager etc. take part in school training on INSET days?

General questions that can be asked of all candidates

- Please detail your experience to date and say what skills and qualities you have developed over that time.
- A parent comes into school at the end of the day being abusive – how would you deal with this?
- In what ways do you see the community being involved in the school?
- What involvement do you foresee having in the life of the school?
- What are your outside interests? Do you feel they could be used for the benefit of pupils?
- What languages do you speak?
- Why have you applied for a post at this school?
- Why should we appoint you?
- (These last two questions would be particularly important in ascertaining whether people would fit into our school team.)

REFERENCES

Athey, C (1981), 'Parental involvement in nursery education'. *Early Child Development and Care*, 7, 4, 253-67.

Bell, G. (1995), 'The Personal Effectiveness Programme Initiative: the comprehensive guide to personal effectiveness for education and business partners' (Chester: Bell).

Black, P and Wiliam, D (1998), *Inside the Black Box: raising standards through classroom assessment*, London: King's College School of Education.

Blanchard, K (1994), *Leadership and the One Minute Manager* (London: HarperCollins).

Buckley, A (2003), *The Kids' Yoga Deck* (San Francisco: Chronicle Books).

Caviglioli, O and Harris, I (2000), *Mapwise* (Stafford: Network Educational Press).

Clarke, S (2001), *Unlocking Formative Assessment* (London: Hodder and Stoughton).

Claxton, G (1999), *Wise Up: the challenge of lifelong learning* (London: Bloomsbury).

CLPE (1988), *The Primary Language Record: handbook for teachers* (London, CLPE).

DES (1985), 'The Curriculum from 5 to 16: Curriculum Matters', Series 2 (London: HMSO).

DfEE (1999), *The National Curriculum: handbook for primary teachers in England* (London: HMSO).

DfES (2003a), 'Every Child Matters: Change for Children' (Nottingham: DfES Publications).

DfES (2003b), 'Excellence and Enjoyment: a strategy for primary schools' (Nottingham: DfES Publications).

DfES (2004a), 'Five-Year Strategy for Children and Learners' (Norwich: HMSO).

DfES (2004b), 'A National Conversation about Personalised Learning' (Nottingham: DfES Publications).

DfES / Ofsted (2004c), 'A New Relationship with Schools' (Nottingham: DfES Publications).

DfES (2005), 'Higher Standards, Better Schools for All – More Choice for Parents and Pupils', White Paper.

Gardner, H (1984), *Frames of Mind* (New York: HarperCollins).

Halpern, S (1985), *Sound Health* (New York: Harper and Row).

Hannan, G (2001), *Strategies for Improving Learning* (CD-ROM and DVD available from www.hannans.org.uk).

Hargreaves, D (2004), 'Transformation through Global Networking, a working conference' conference paper, Melbourne, Australia, July 26–8.

Jensen, E P (2000), *Brain-Based Learning* (revised edition) (San Diego, CA: The Brain Store).

Leadbeater, C (2004), 'Learning about Personalisation: how can we put the learner at the heart of the education system?' (Nottingham: DfES publications).

Lucas, B (2001), *Power Up Your Mind* (London: Nicholas Brearley Publishing).

Lucas, B, and Smith, A (2002), *Help Your Child to Succeed – the essential guide for parents* (Stafford: Network Educational Press).

Mosley, J (1998), *Quality Circle Time in the Primary Classroom* (Wisbech, Cambs: LDA).

Open University (1980), *Curriculum in Action: practical classroom evaluation* (Milton Keynes: Open University Press).

Piaget, J and Inhelder, B (1969), *The Psychology of the Child* (London: Routledge and Kegan Paul).

QCA / DfEE (2000), 'Curriculum Guidance for the Foundation Stage' (London: QCA).

Smith, A (1996), *Accelerated Learning in the Classroom* (Stafford: Network Educational Press).

Sure Start (2003), 'Birth to Three Matters: a framework to support children in their earliest years' (London: Sure Start Unit).

Webb, D, and Webb, T (1990), *Accelerated Learning with Music* (Norcross, GA: Accelerated Learning Systems).

INDEX